Hemispheres 3

**Scott Cameron
Susan Iannuzzi
Mary Ann Maynard**

Edward J. Scarry

Hemispheres 3 Student Book

Published by McGraw-Hill ESL/ELT, a business unit of The McGraw-Hill Companies, Inc., 1221 Avenue of the Americas, New York, NY 10020. Copyright © 2008 by The McGraw-Hill Companies, Inc. All rights reserved. No part of this publication may be reproduced or distributed in any form or by any means, or stored in a database or retrieval system, without the prior written consent of The McGraw-Hill Companies, Inc., including, but not limited to, in any network or other electronic storage or transmission, or broadcast for distance learning.

ISBN 13: 978-0-07-719103-0 (Student Book with Audio Highlights)
ISBN 10: 0-07-719103-X
1 2 3 4 5 6 7 8 9 10 QWC 11 10 09 08 07

Editorial director: Tina Carver
Series editor: Annie Sullivan
Senior development editors: Amy Lawler, Annie Sullivan
Production manager: Juanita Thompson
Production coordinator: James D. Gwyn
Cover Designer: Wee Design Group
Reading and chart designs: Cynthia Malaran
Interior designer: Nesbitt Graphics, Inc.
Artists: Scott Burroughs, Kanako Damerum, Mark Divico, Nadia Simard, Yuzuru Takasaki
Photo researcher: Antonina Smith

The credits section for this book begins on page 151 and is considered an extension of the copyright page.

Cover photo: © Farinaz Taghavi/Corbis

Hemispheres 3 Components

Student Book with Audio Highlights
Workbook
Teacher's Manual
Audio CDs
DVD
DVD Workbook
EZ Test® CD-ROM Test Generator

www.esl.mcgraw-hill.com

The McGraw·Hill Companies

ACKNOWLEDGMENTS

The authors and publisher would like to thank the following teachers, program directors, and teacher trainers, who reviewed the *Hemispheres* program at various stages of development and whose comments, reviews, and field-testing were instrumental in helping us shape the series:

Dee Parker, Jeffrey Taschner, **American University Alumni Language Center,** Bangkok, Thailand
David Scholz, **AUA- Rajadamri Branch,** Bangkok, Thailand
Snow White O. Smelser, **AUA- Ratchayothin,** Bangkok, Thailand
Anthony Pavia, Dr. Joseph W. Southern, **AUA-Srinikarin,** Bangkok, Thailand
Maria Adele Ryan, Maria Teresa de la Torre Aranda, **Associação Alumni,** São Paulo, Brazil
Lúcia Catharina Bodeman Campos, **Associação Brasil-América (ABA),** Pernambuco, Brazil
Marissa Araquistain, Gabriel Areas, Douglas Arroliga, Francisco Hodgson, Maria Mora, Aleyda Reyes, Jairo Rivar, Gloria Tunnerman, Sarah Walsh, **Ave Maria College of the Americas,** Managua, Nicaragua
Bruce Avasadanand, **Bangkok School of Management,** Bangkok, Thailand
Yanan Une-aree, **Bangkok University,** Bangkok, Thailand
Suchada Rattanawanitpun, **Burapha University,** Chon Buri, Thailand
Isabela de Freitas Villas Boas, Catherine Taliaferro Cox, **Casa Thomas Jefferson,** Brasilia, Brazil
Fernando Trevino, **Centro de Idiomas,** Monterrey, Mexico
Maria Zavala, **Centro Educativo los Pinos,** Guadalajara, Mexico
Karen Pereira Meneses, **Centro Educativo Yurusti,** Costa Rica
Wuyen Wayne Ni, **Chung Kuo Institute of Technology and Commerce,** Taipei, Taiwan
Mónica González, **Colegio InterCanadiense de Puebla,** A.C, Puebla, Mexico
Rosa Ma. Chacon, Henry Angulo Jiménez, Johannia Piedra, **Colegio Saleciano Don Bosco,** San Jose, Costa Rica
Marjorie Friedman, **ELS Language Centers,** Florida, United States
Joseph Dziver, **Florida State University** - English Language Program, Panama
Raymond Kao, **Fu Hsing Kang College,** Taipei, Taiwan
Marie J. Guilloteaux, **Gyeongsang National University,** Jinju, Korea
Jana Opicic, **Harvest English Institute,** New Jersey, United States
Wilma Luth, **Hokusei Gakuen University,** Sapporo, Japan
Daniela Alves Meyer, José Manuel da Silva, Maria do Socorro Guimarães, **Instituto Brasil-Estados Unidos (IBEU),** Rio de Janeiro, Brazil
Rosario Garcia Alfonso, **Instituto Copernico,** Guadalajara, Mexico
Nefertiti Gonzales, **Instituto Mexicano Madero,** Puebla, Mexico
Rosa Isabel de la Garza, Elvira Marroquin Medina, **Instituto Regiomontano,** Monterrey, Mexico
Robert van Trieste, **Inter American University of Puerto Rico,** San Juan, Puerto Rico
Elisabeth Lindgren, Annetta Stroud, **Intrax International Institute,** California, United States
Tracy Cramer, **Kansai Gaidai University,** Osaka, Japan
Lilliam Quesada Solano, **Licco Experimental Bilingue Jose Figueres,** Cartago, Costa Rica
Paul Cameron, **National Chengchi University,** Taipei, Taiwan
Elsa Fan, **National Chiao Tung University,** Taipei, Taiwan
Jessie Huang, **National Central University,** Taipei, Taiwan
Marcia Monica A. Saiz, **Naval Academy,** Brazil
Pamela Vittorio, **New School University,** New York, United States
Steve Cornwell, **Osaka Jogakuin College,** Osaska, Japan
Kathryn Aparicio, Inda Shirley, **San Francisco Institute of English,** California, United States
Dan Neal, **Shih Chien University,** Taipei, Taiwan
Kevin Miller, **Shikoku University,** Tokushima, Japan
Mark Brown, Linda Sky Emerson, Jinyoung Hong, Young-Ok Kim, **Sogang University,** Seoul, Korea
Colin Gullberg, **Soochow University,** Taipei, Taiwan
Michael Martin, Juthumas Sukontha, **Sripatum University,** Bangkok, Thailand
Damian Benstead, Roy Langdon, **Sungkyunkwan University,** Seoul, Korea
Cheryl Magnant, Jeff Moore, Devon Scoble, **Sungkyunkwan University,** Seoul, Korea
Raymond Kao, Taiwan **Military University,** Taipei, Taiwan
Dr. Saneh Thongrin, **Thammasat University,** Bangkok, Thailand
Patrick Kiernan, **Tokyo Denki University,** Tokyo, Japan
Yoshiko Matsubayashi, **Tokyo International University,** Saitama, Japan
Mike Hood, Patrick McCoy, **Tokyo University,** Tokyo, Japan
Rafael Cárdenas, Victoria Peralta, Isaac Secaida, Roy Tejeira, **UDELAS - Centro Inteligente de Lenguas de Las Américas,** Panama
Olga Chaves Carballo, **ULACIT,** San Jose, Costa Rica
Adela de Maria y Campos, **Unidades Básicas UPAEP,** Puebla, Mexico
Olda C. de Arauz, **Universidad Autonoma de Chiriqui,** Panama
Ignacio Yepez, **Universidad Autonoma de Guadalajara,** Guadalajara, Mexico
Yohanna Abarca Amador, Cesar Navas Brenes, Gabriela Cerdas, Elisa Li Chan, Ligia de Coto, Maria Eugenia Flores, Carlos Navarro, Johanna Piedra, Allen Quesada-Pacheco, Mary Scholl, Karen Solis, Alonso Canales Viquez, **Universidad de Costa Rica,** San Jose, Costa Rica
John Ball, Geraldine Torack-Durán, **Universidad de las Américas, A.C.,** Mexico City, Mexico
Victoria Lee, **Universidad del Istmo,** Panama
Ramiro Padilla Muñoz, Sandra Hernandez Salazar, **Universidad del Valle de Atemajac (UNIVA),** Guadalajara, Mexico
Alan Heaberlin, Sophia Holder, **Universidad Interamericana,** San Jose, Costa Rica
Fraser Smith, Michael Werner, **Universidad Latina,** Costa Rica
Gilberto Hernàndez, **Universidad Metropolitana Castro Carazo,** Alajuela, Costa Rica
Angela Calderon, **Universidad Santa Maria La Antigua,** Panama
Edith Espino, **Universidad Tecnológica de Panamá,** Panama
Thomas Riedmiller, **University of Northern Iowa,** Iowa, United States
Stella M. Aneiro, Ivette Delgado, Prof. Marisol Santiago Pérez, Ida Roman, **University of Puerto Rico - Arecibo,** Puerto Rico
Aida Caceres, **University of Puerto Rico - Humacao,** Humacao, Puerto Rico
Regino Megill, **University of Puerto Rico - Ponce,** Ponce, Puerto Rico
Dr. Emily Krasinski, **University of Puerto Rico,** San Juan, Puerto Rico

TO THE TEACHER

WELCOME TO HEMISPHERES

Hemispheres is a four-level integrated skills series for adults and young adults that puts skills-building back into integrated skills! The course is designed both for students studying general English and for those studying English with a view toward more academic work. The series strategically develops both language skills and critical thinking skills. The thought-provoking topics and appealing, user-friendly design invite learners to enter into the skills development without hesitation.

FEATURES

- **Balance of language areas:** Reading, listening, speaking, writing, and grammar are balanced and integrated throughout the unit.
- **Academic skills:** A variety of activities ensures the purposeful development of academic skills, such as summarizing, paraphrasing, making predictions, identifying gist, and using graphs to aid comprehension.
- **Critical thinking skills:** The consistent focus on essential critical thinking skills encourages independent thinking and learning. These critical thinking skills include analyzing, synthesizing, making inferences, understanding organization, and drawing conclusions.
- **TOEFL® iBT:** Each unit helps to build readiness for the TOEFL® iBT. The Put It to the Test section includes reading and listening activities followed by TOEFL® iBT type questions that include personal interpretation, independent speaking and writing, and integrated speaking and writing.
- **Grammar expansion activities:** Additional grammar practice activities for each unit reinforce learning.
- **High interest content:** Unusual, attention-grabbing topics generate discussion and offer opportunities for students to express their own opinions.
- **DVD and DVD Workbook:** The DVD illustrates conversation strategies and critical thinking skills in an engaging storyline, and the accompanying DVD Workbook ensures comprehension and encourages additional open-ended application of the critical thinking skills.
- **Student book with audio highlights:** Students can listen to dialogues multiple times with the audio for additional individual practice.
- **Recycling:** Content and language are continuously and consistently recycled with variations to lead the learner from receptive to creative language production.

COMPONENTS FOR LEVEL 3

- Student Book with audio highlights
- Interleaved Teacher's Book
- Workbook
- Audio CDs
- DVD
- DVD Workbook
- EZ Test® CD-ROM with Test Generator

*TOEFL is a registered trademark of Educational Testing Service (ETS). This publication is not endorsed or approved by ETS.

PUTTING THE SKILLS BACK INTO THE FOUR-SKILLS COURSE

Hemispheres has put the skills-building back into the four-skills course. It supports students in the development of language skills, while at the same time emphasizing critical thinking skills. Reading, listening, speaking, and writing skills are purposefully developed in ways that are similar to single skill books. Helpful Skill Focus boxes make the skills development information manageable and give students practical guidance that they can use throughout the book or as a reference.

Critical Thinking Skills

Hemispheres features critical thinking skills development together with language skills development. Students are encouraged to take charge of their learning and to become independent thinkers. Activities ask students to make inferences, analyze, synthesize, and understand the relationships between ideas.

Integrating the Skills

Hemispheres carefully integrates skills in both presentations and practice. Meaningful speaking activities and role-plays are integrated with reading and listening. Relevant reading models are integrated with writing. Grammar is practiced through thematically related reading, listening, speaking, and writing. Opportunities abound for students to personalize the activities throughout the series.

Put It to the Test and TOEFL® iBT

Hemispheres builds valuable test taking skills while recycling critical thinking skills in the Put It to the Test section of each unit. A strategic pairing of reading and listening requires that students analyze or synthesize information to understand how the two are related. The reading may present a theory, while the listening provides examples supporting that theory; the reading may explain a problem, while the listening provides a solution to the problem; the reading may present an argument, while the listening presents a counterargument; or the reading and listening may present different points of view. The readings and listenings are short and thematically related to the unit, and they are followed by comprehension checkpoints. Students are asked TOEFL® iBT style questions which require them to identify the relationship between the ideas in the reading and those in the listening. They then have an opportunity to discuss and personalize the topic in this section.

DVD

Shot in high-definition, the DVD features six young adults who live in New York City. In addition to showing conversation strategies and critical thinking skills in real-life contexts, the DVD recycles the vocabulary and grammar presented in the student books.

Correlations

Hemispheres is correlated to the TOEFL®iBT, TOEIC® examination, and CEF. It provides solid preparation for students whose instructional needs are linked to any of these instruments.

SCOPE AND SEQUENCE

Unit	Reading	Listening	Grammar
Unit 1 The Other Side of Fame Page 2	■ Scanning for specific information ★ Reading for answers to *wh-* questions	■ Listening for specific information ★ Comparing and contrasting	■ Questions in the simple present and simple past ■ Quantifiers *no, some, a lot of, a whole lot of, most of (the), a few, many, a little*
Unit 2 Scents Page 12	■ Skimming for the main idea ★ Sequencing	★ Listening for gist ■ Identifying examples to support your answer	■ Review the simple present, present continuous, simple past, and past continuous
Unit 3 Relating Page 22	■ Using titles and headings to aid comprehension ★ Making inferences	■ Listening to confirm first impressions ★ Using prior knowledge and impressions to make predictions	■ Gerunds and infinitives: differences in meanings following *stop, remember, forget*
Unit 4 Digging Page 32	■ Skimming for the main idea ★ Understanding what pronouns refer to	★ Anticipating topic and language from context and visual aids ★ Getting basic information without understanding every word	■ Dependent and independent clauses
Unit 5 Creating an Image Page 42	★ Understanding parenthetical information ■ Reading for specific information	■ Listening for specific information ★ Listening to distinguish between fact and opinion	■ Simple present for future
Unit 6 Things that Scare Us Page 52	■ Scanning to see what information is included in a text ★ Identifying words that indicate purpose	■ Identifying correct information ★ Recognizing supporting examples	■ Quantifiers: *a few, few, a little,* and *little*

★ Critical thinking skill

Vocabulary	Conversation Strategy	Writing	TOEFL® iBT Focus
- anonymous, celebrity, exhausting, idol, look up to, overrated, privacy, underrated	- Asking for and giving advice	- Mastering the parts of a paragraph	- Reading for factual information - Reading for inference - Listening for gist—content - Listening for purpose - Independent writing
- condition, cope, face challenges, fragrance, incident, odor, permanent, senses, take precautions, temporary	- Asking for additional information	- Writing topic sentences	- Reading for negative facts - Reading for vocabulary - Listening for gist—purpose - Listening to understand stance - Independent speaking
- aggressive, amazing, antisocial, compassionate, exhausting, frustrated, gentle, good-natured, patient	- Commiserating	- Using graphic organizers for planning	- Reading for rhetorical purpose - Reading for reference - Listening for detail - Listening for inference about content - Integrated writing
- Suffixes for occupations: *artist, cartoonist, chemist, columnist, cyclist, economist, environmentalist, geologist, linguist, psychiatrist, receptionist, violinist*	- Correcting a misinterpretation	- Using descriptive language	- Reading with sentence insertions - Reading for inference - Listening for gist—purpose - Listening for inference - Listening for sequence - Integrated speaking
- come up with, exposure, logo, memorable, pay off, promote, slogan	- Asking and answering personal questions	- Supporting your writing with graphs and charts	- Reading to summarize - Reading for vocabulary - Listening for gist—content - Listening for rhetorical strategies - Independent writing
- confident, depressed, gradually, patient, thrilling, treatment, unbearable, virtual	- Asking if someone has time to talk	- Using punctuation to convey tone or emotion	- Reading for specific information - Reading for reference - Listening for detail - Listening for purpose - Independent speaking

SCOPE AND SEQUENCE

Unit	Reading	Listening	Grammar
Unit 7 Transformations Page 62	■ Making inferences ★ Paraphrasing	■ Listening for specific information ★ Sequencing	■ The past perfect and the simple past
Unit 8 Frozen Page 72	■ Confirming predictions ★ Summarizing	■ Listening for specific information ★ Using context clues to infer a speaker's feelings	■ Modals of possibility: *could, may, might*
Unit 9 Brains Page 82	★ Distinguishing between fact and opinion ★ Identifying a writer's point of view	■ Listening for specific information ★ Drawing a conclusion	■ Restrictive adjective clauses
Unit 10 Keeping Secrets Page 92	■ Scanning for specific information ★ Making inferences based on written and visual information	■ Identifying true and false information ★ Evaluating advantages (pros) and disadvantages (cons)	■ The passive verb form
Unit 11 Sleeping and Dreaming Page 102	■ Scanning for specific information ★ Identifying cause and effect	■ Listening to confirm predictions ★ Making inferences	■ Future real conditional
Unit 12 Movies Page 112	■ Scanning for specific information ★ Relating to content as you read	■ Identifying original speakers in a conversation of reported speech ★ Restating information.	■ Reported speech

★ Critical thinking skill

Vocabulary	Conversation Strategy	Writing	TOEFL® iBT Focus
■ blame, coincidentally, encounter, impact, thriving, transform, triumphantly, vibrant	■ Getting to the point	■ Maintaining verb tense consistency	■ Reading for essential information ■ Reading for inference ■ Listening for gist—content ■ Listening to understand stance ■ Integrated writing
■ demanding, having a blast, opportunity, sick of, staff, tiny, was dying to	■ Expressing tentative agreement	■ Writing more effective summaries	■ Reading for factual information ■ Reading for vocabulary ■ Listening for gist—purpose ■ Listening for inference about content ■ Integrated speaking
■ Prefixes: *im-, in-,* and *un-* impossible, incapable, inconsistent, incorrect, unacceptable, unclear, unethical, unfair	■ Making excuses	■ Introducing additional information to expand on an idea	■ Reading for rhetorical purpose ■ Reading for reference ■ Listening for detail ■ Listening to connect content ■ Independent writing
■ at risk, compromised, confidential, detect, disgusts, get rid of, handle, turned upside down	■ Ending a conversation	■ Writing a character description	■ Reading to details ■ Reading for inference ■ Listening for purpose ■ Listening for gist—content ■ Independent speaking
■ assassinate, grieve, guidance, inspire, organic chemistry, premonition, reveal, scripture, significant	■ Showing that you are paying attention	■ Writing about cause and effect	■ Reading for essential information ■ Reading for vocabulary ■ Listening for gist—purpose ■ Listening for purpose ■ Integrated writing
■ angles, aspects, build, cast, crew, fill in, headset, punching	■ Speculating	■ Using introductory clauses with *although, even though,* and *while*	■ Reading to summarize ■ Reading for reference ■ Listening for detail ■ Listening to understand stance ■ Integrated speaking

HIGHLIGHTS OF HEMISPHERES 3

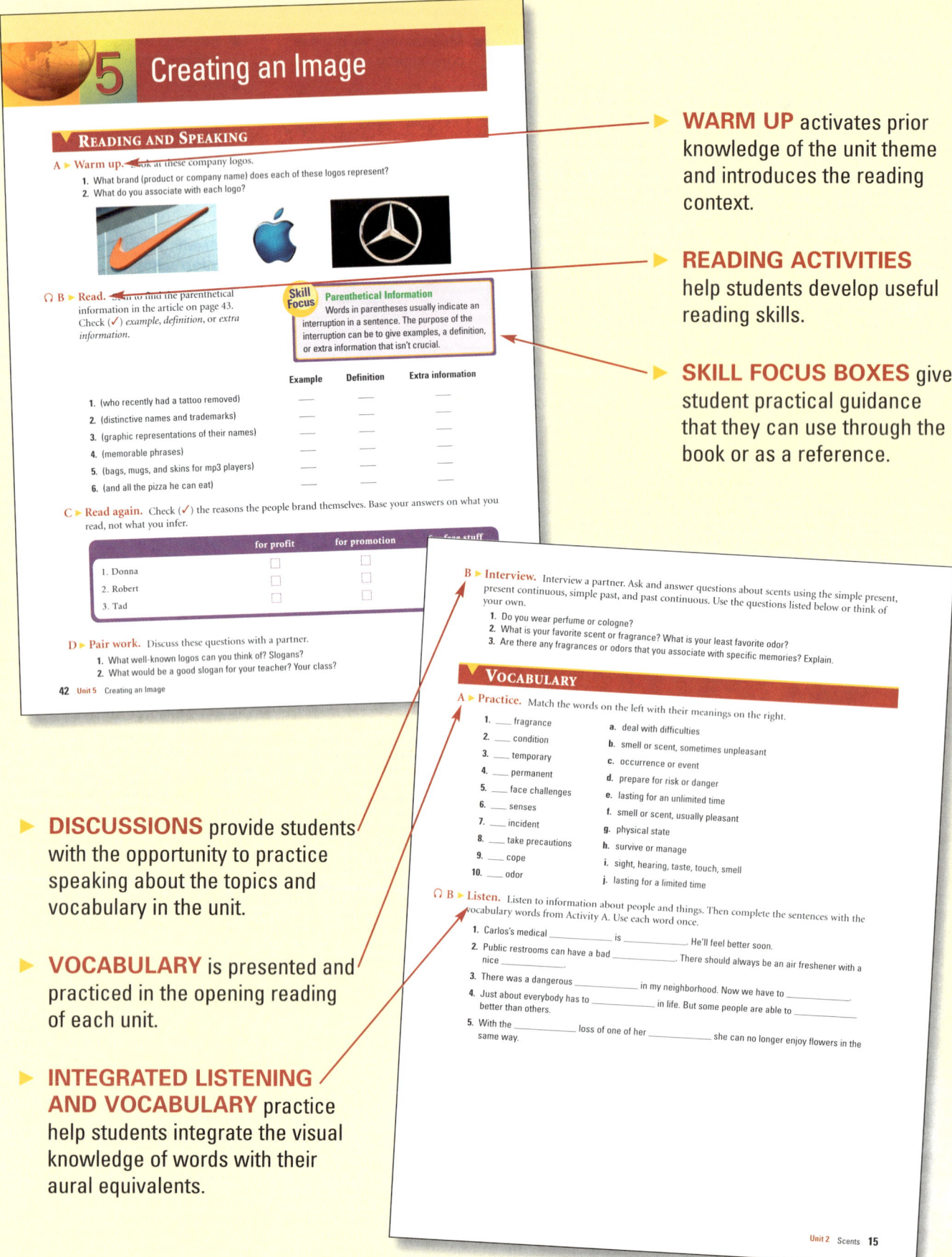

► **WARM UP** activates prior knowledge of the unit theme and introduces the reading context.

► **READING ACTIVITIES** help students develop useful reading skills.

► **SKILL FOCUS BOXES** give student practical guidance that they can use through the book or as a reference.

► **DISCUSSIONS** provide students with the opportunity to practice speaking about the topics and vocabulary in the unit.

► **VOCABULARY** is presented and practiced in the opening reading of each unit.

► **INTEGRATED LISTENING AND VOCABULARY** practice help students integrate the visual knowledge of words with their aural equivalents.

- **GRAMMAR** explanation and examples serve as a reference for students.

- **GUIDED PRACTICE** includes controlled practice of the grammar or an error correction exercise. Grammar expansion exercises at the end of the book provide more practice for each unit.

- **INTEGRATED LISTENING AND GRAMMAR ACTIVITIES** allow students to experience the grammar in real language through meaningful, thematically related listening activities.

- **PREDICTION** activities encourage students to anticipate content in the listenings and readings.

- **A VARIETY OF LISTENING COMPREHENSION ACTIVITIES** establish a solid base of listening competency in students.

- **CRITICAL LISTENING SKILLS** build students' comprehension ability with more challenging listening experiences. Skills include listening for gist, identifying tone, distinguishing between pros and cons, identifying cause and effect relationships, and sequencing.

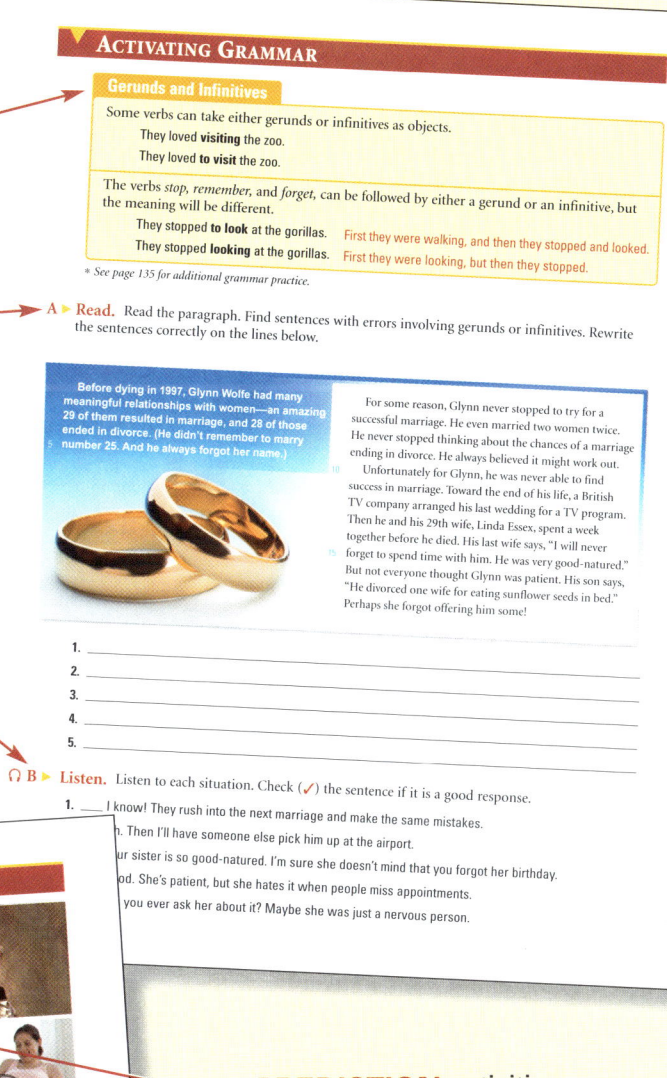

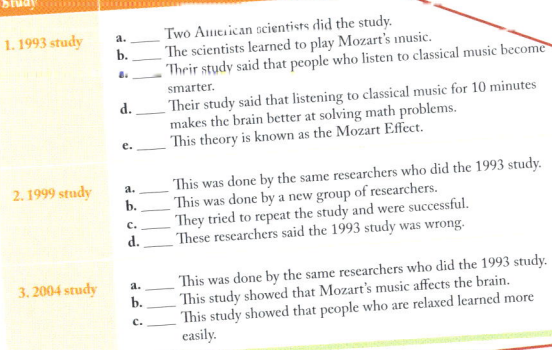

xi

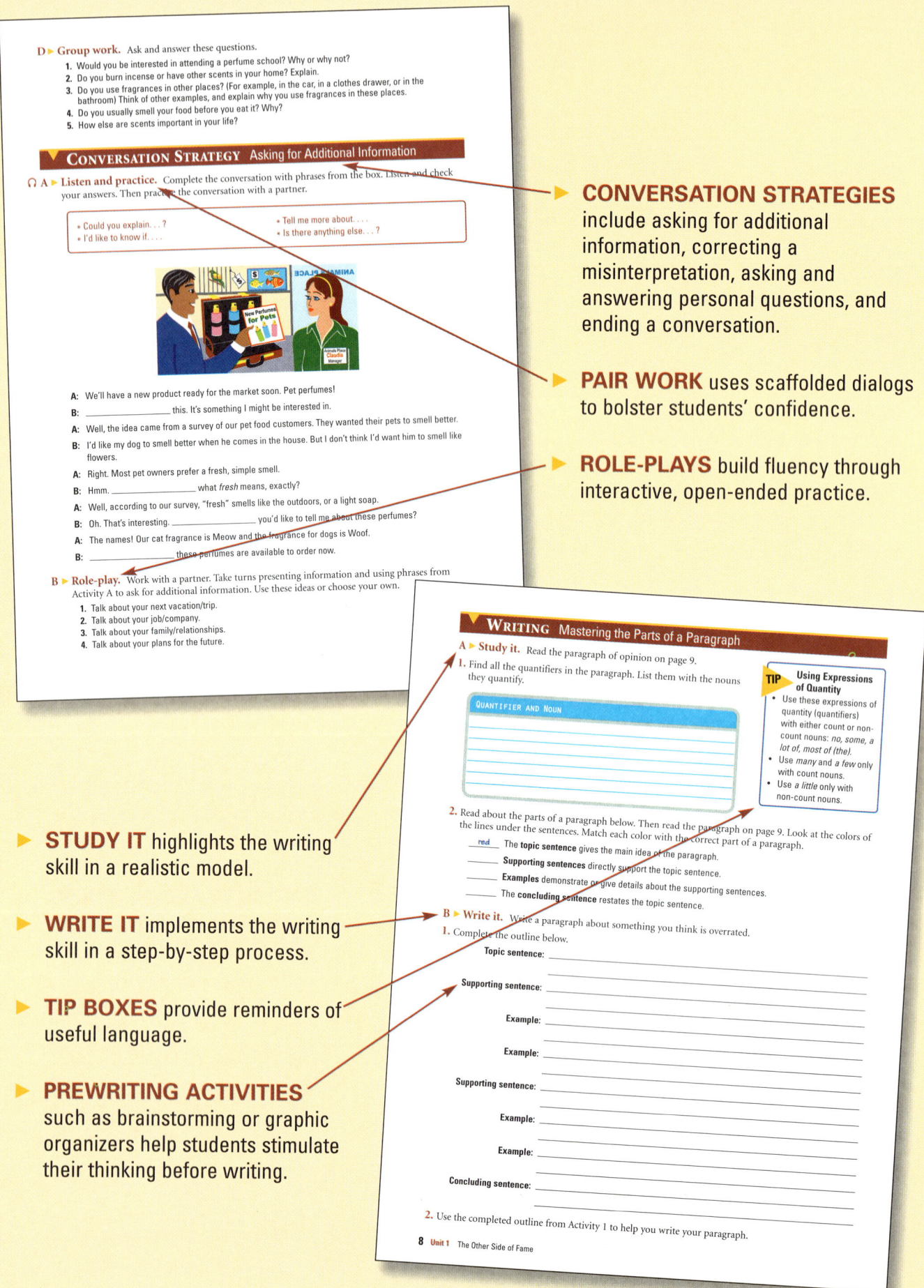

▶ **CONVERSATION STRATEGIES** include asking for additional information, correcting a misinterpretation, asking and answering personal questions, and ending a conversation.

▶ **PAIR WORK** uses scaffolded dialogs to bolster students' confidence.

▶ **ROLE-PLAYS** build fluency through interactive, open-ended practice.

▶ **STUDY IT** highlights the writing skill in a realistic model.

▶ **WRITE IT** implements the writing skill in a step-by-step process.

▶ **TIP BOXES** provide reminders of useful language.

▶ **PREWRITING ACTIVITIES** such as brainstorming or graphic organizers help students stimulate their thinking before writing.

xii

▶ **PUT IT TO THE TEST** helps students find out if they have learned the content of the unit.

▶ **THE STRATEGIC PAIRING OF READING AND LISTENING** in Put It to the Test requires students to analyze or synthesize information. This builds valuable test-taking skills while recycling critical thinking skills.

▶ **TOEFL® IBT** type questions help students prepare for the test.

PUT IT TO THE TEST

A ▶ Read.

1. Read the article. Then answer the questions that follow.

Brain Fingerprinting

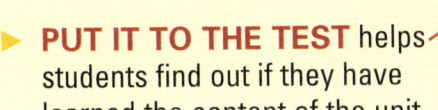

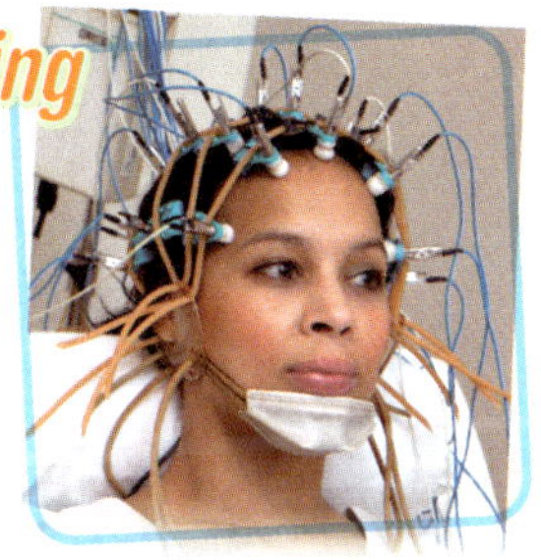

Terry Harrington was convicted of murder in 1978 and was serving a life sentence in prison. Throughout his imprisonment, he said he was innocent. In 2003, he was released from prison and is now a free man. He can thank his memory and a new technology called brain fingerprinting for his freedom.

Clues to innocence or guilt are found in the brain. Perpetrators (people who commit a crime) have details of the crime stored in their memory. Brain Fingerprinting Laboratories, Inc. has developed technology that determines whether or not specific information is stored in a person's memory. The test measures brain wave responses to pictures or words associated with the crime scene. When the human brain recognizes certain information, it triggers a specific electrical signal called a MERMER. This signal can be measured and analyzed to prove whether the suspect has the crime in his memory. Since an innocent person did not commit the crime, no memory of it will be found in the brain. The murder that Terry Harrington was wrongly convicted for took place in a field with high grass and tall weeds. The results of Terry's brain fingerprinting test showed that the record stored in his brain did not match the crime scene but it did match his alibi of being at a concert the night of the murder.

Polygraphs (lie detectors) measure physical and emotional reactions to questions. Increases in pulse, blood pressure, breathing rate, and sweat levels are believed to be signs of guilt. Critics of polygraphs say that some people can trick the lie detector while nervous people could be seen as guilty. During a brain fingerprinting test, pictures or words from the crime scene come up on a computer screen. If this same information is stored in the person's memory, the brain will recognize it, whether the person wants to or not. The brain wave will be the sign of memory.

Sources: Accessed March 2007 at http://www.brainwavescience.com/ExecutiveSummary.php; Accessed March 2007 at http://www.brainwavescience.com/NewYorkTimes.php; Accessed March 2007 at http://www.brainwavescience.com/CBS%2060%20Min%20High.php

2. Answer these questions about the reading.

1. The author discusses Terry Harrington's murder case in order to
   a. show that brain fingerprinting has helped free innocent people
   b. demonstrate the reliability of brain fingerprinting
   c. show that brain fingerprinting doesn't work
   d. support Terry Harrington

2. Why does the author mention polygraphs?
   a. To show that brain fingerprinting is comparable to polygraphs
   b. To explain that polygraphs are more reliable than brain fingerprinting
   c. To show that polygraphs are not as effective as brain fingerprinting
   d. To introduce another tool that is just as effective as brain fingerprinting

3. The word *it* in line 19 refers to
   a. the signal
   b. the crime
   c. the brain
   d. the memory

90 Unit 9 Brains

---

3. The word *more* in the passage refers to _____.
   a. skits
   b. videos
   c. friends
   d. vloggers

🎧 B ▶ Listen.

Listen to part of a conversation between two friends. You may take notes as you listen. Then answer the questions.

1. What is the man's son doing?
   a. Making videos to put on YouTube
   b. Spending too much time on YouTube
   c. Watching too much TV
   d. Spending too much time on e-mail

2. According to the woman, vloggers make videos that are all _____.
   a. short
   b. funny
   c. bad
   d. expensive

3. What can be inferred about the man?
   a. He doesn't know much about using the Internet.
   b. He has trouble understanding how computers work.
   c. He doesn't want to get involved in his son's life.
   d. He wants to ban his son from watching YouTube.

C ▶ Personal interpretation.

Try to imagine the entertainment business 10 years in the future. In what ways might video-sharing Websites, such as YouTube, change the movie and TV industry? Prepare a two-minute spoken response to this question.

D ▶ Integrated speaking.

Prepare a response to the following question. You will have 20 seconds to prepare and 60 seconds to give your response.

In the listening section, two people discuss possible solutions to the man's problem. Describe the problem. Then state which of the two solutions you prefer and explain why.

Unit 12 Movies 121

▶ **LISTENING** activities mimic the type of listening passages and questions found on the TOEFL© iBT test.

▶ **PERSONAL INTERPRETATION** provides the opportunity for students to personalize information under discussion by making connections with their own lives.

▶ **INTEGRATED SPEAKING** gives students practice in reflecting upon a reading or listening passage and then speaking about it with a test-like time constraint.

xiii

1 The Other Side of Fame

READING AND SPEAKING

A ▶ Warm up. Read the title of the article on page 3, and look at the picture. How do you think a personal assistant's job is different from the job of an assistant in an office?

B ▶ Read. Scan the article for answers to the questions.

1. What is Rebecca Tan's first rule of being a celebrity's personal assistant?
   _____

2. What is her book about? _____

3. Was Rebecca paid well as a celebrity personal assistant?
   _____

4. Why does Rebecca refuse to name horrible celebrities she knows?
   _____

C ▶ Read again. Write seven wh- questions from the article. Then work with a partner. Ask the questions, and give the answers you find in the reading.

1. _____
2. _____
3. _____
4. _____
5. _____
6. _____
7. _____

> **Skill Focus: Reading for Answers to Wh- Questions**
>
> In an interview, many questions are asked and answered. Stay alert for questions beginning with wh- question words: who, what, where, when, why, and how. Key information is often contained in the answers.

D ▶ Pair work. Discuss these questions with a partner.

1. Would you like to be a celebrity's personal assistant? Why or why not?
2. Imagine that you could have an assistant. What might your assistant do for you?

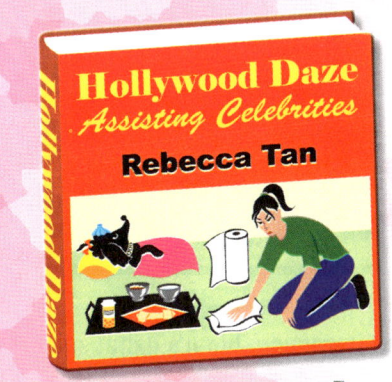

Assistant to the Stars

Our correspondent, Chad Lee, interviews Rebecca Tan, Director of Celebrity Personal Assistants Training.

Lee: So, Rebecca, you train personal assistants for celebrities. What do you teach your trainees?

Tan: Rule number one: Respect the celebrity's privacy. If you can't keep a secret, you won't keep your job! Never tell others who you work for or what you do.

Lee: Why is privacy so important?

Tan: Because celebrities don't like reading about their personal lives in magazines!

Lee: How can people research this job, then? They can't talk to the people doing it....

Tan: They can talk to us. And to people who were assistants in the past. They can also read my book. I was a celebrity assistant for 25 years.

Lee: When did your book come out?

Tan: In 2007. It's about the responsibilities of the job. But I warn your readers—they may discover the job's overrated. I describe things like waking up at four A.M. to clean up after a celebrity's sick dog and then working until late the next night.

Lee: That sounds disgusting... and exhausting! Why did you stay for 25 years?

Tan: The job paid well, and I met some of my Hollywood idols. I also met some celebrities I could look up to—good people who treat others well.

Lee: Do you think most celebrities are good people?

Tan: Yes. Some celebrities are horrible, but others are underrated, as people. For example, singer Tom Waits is great. I once wrote him a letter, telling him how much I admired the way he treats his fans, his staff, and the public. But I decided not to send it—I didn't want him to think I was looking for a job. I guess I could have sent it anonymously—but, I didn't think of it. Anyway, I still really admire him.

Lee: Who are some horrible celebrities?

Tan: I can't name the horrible ones.

Lee: Why can't you name them?

Tan: I'd be breaking rule number 1!

LISTENING

Listen to Ellen Chew talk about working for a famous model. Check (✓) the things the model did.

___ threw her purse at Ellen

___ paid the vet bills for Ellen's dog

___ threw her cell phone at Ellen

___ sent concert tickets to Ellen's sister

___ sent flowers to Ellen's sister

___ gave Ellen money to buy a TV

Unit 1 The Other Side of Fame **3**

ACTIVATING GRAMMAR

Questions in the Simple Present and Simple Past

Questions in the simple present or simple past that begin with a form of the verb *be* or *do* can be answered with *yes* or *no*. Wh- questions ask *who? what? where? when?* or *why?* and require more specific answers. (Note: *How* is also included with Wh- questions.)

Yes/No Questions in the Simple Present	Answers
Is it easy to be a celebrity personal assistant?	No. It**'s** interesting, but it**'s** exhausting.
Do you **like** living in Hollywood?	Yes, I **do**. It**'s** an exciting place to live.
Yes/No Questions in the Simple Past	Answers
Were you able to get this job easily?	No, not really. It **took** a long time.
Did you **have** a job before this one?	No. I **was** a student.
Wh- Questions in the Simple Present	Answers
Who do you **admire** most?	My dad, actually. I still **look up** to him.
Where does he live now?	He **lives** in Dallas, Texas.
How do you **spend** your free time?	I **stay home**. I **enjoy** the peace and privacy.
Wh- Questions in the Simple Past	Answers
What did you study in college?	English and communications.
When did you start your current job?	I **started** over 25 years ago!
Why did you decide to go professional?	Because of the pay. The money is great.

* *See page 135 for additional grammar practice.*

A ▶ Read. Complete the questions in the interview below with Jason Raleigh, who recently became a professional baseball celebrity.

Q: Jason, you're a celebrity now. _____ your life easier these days?

A: No. I thought it would be easier. But it's hard on my family.

Q: _____?

A: Because I have no privacy. People follow me everywhere. Yesterday I was at the supermarket with my wife,
5   and a woman asked me to autograph her car.

Q: _____ did you do?

A: I did what she wanted me to. And then she invited me to a party!

Q: _____ you accept her
10 invitation?

A: No! Why would I? I don't know her.

Q: So, _____ *do* you spend your free time?

A: I try to spend time with my wife and children,
15 away from my fans.

4 Unit 1 The Other Side of Fame

B ▶ Role-play. Work with a partner. Read the situation below. Work together to write interview questions and answers. Include both *yes/no* and *wh-* questions. Then act out the interview.
1. One of you is the assistant to a successful businessperson.
2. One of you is a reporter interviewing the assistant for a newspaper article.

VOCABULARY

A ▶ Practice. Complete the sentences with words from the box.

anonymous	celebrity	exhausting	idol
look up to	overrated	privacy	underrated

1. My younger brothers _____ me. I feel like I have to behave responsibly because they admire me so much. They want to be like me!
2. My job is great, but it's _____! I have a crazy schedule. I have to get up at 5:00 A.M., and I never get enough sleep.
3. Gwen Stefani is my _____. She can write songs, sing, and design clothes.
4. Famous actors shouldn't expect to have _____. They make their money from being popular! People naturally want to know about them.
5. Before winning *American Idol*, Kelly Clarkson was completely _____. No one knew her name! Now she is a _____. She's famous all over the world.
6. I think Gwyneth Paltrow is _____ as an actor. She's only made a few good movies. Most of her parts have been very boring.
7. Most comedy actors are _____. Ben Stiller, Jack Black, and Will Ferrell are very talented. They should win more awards.

B ▶ Listen. Listen to a conversation about a new television show, *Idol of America*, and check (✓) True or False for each sentence.

　　　　　　　　　　　　　　　　　　　　　　　　　　　　　True　False
1. The show's contestants are anonymous.　　　　　　　　□　　□
2. People usually respect the contestants' privacy.　　　　□　　□
3. All the winners of *Idol of America* become celebrities.　□　　□
4. According to Janice, JJ Sharpes was overrated.　　　　□　　□
5. According to Janice, being a judge is underrated.　　　□　　□
6. It's exhausting to be a judge.　　　　　　　　　　　　□　　□

Unit 1　The Other Side of Fame　5

LISTENING Being an Idol

A ▶ Discuss. Look at the picture and make inferences about these two *Idol of America* winners. Which one do you think sang in a rock band in high school? Which one do you think sang in church?

B ▶ Listen. Listen to the interview with two *Idol of America* champions, Joey and Dee. For each sentence, circle the correct answer.

1. Joey thinks being famous is _____.
   a. fun   b. difficult   c. annoying

2. Dee went on *Idol of America* because _____.
   a. she wanted to be a celebrity   b. her friends signed her up   c. she needed money

3. For Joey, the two best things about winning are _____.
   a. fans and having money   b. fans and being famous   c. vacations and friends

4. For Dee, the two best things about winning are _____.
   a. fans and having money   b. having money and doing what she loves   c. fame and fans

5. Which champion likes working more than anything else? _____.
   a. Joey   b. neither   c. Dee

C ▶ Listen again. Compare and contrast. Check (✓) Joey, Dee, or both.

	Joey	Dee
1. worked in a supermarket	☐	☐
2. likes being famous	☐	☐
3. worked in a restaurant	☐	☐
4. had a rock band	☐	☐
5. sang at church	☐	☐
6. wants to buy a house	☐	☐
7. too busy to date	☐	☐
8. wants to take a vacation	☐	☐

Skill Focus: Comparing and Contrasting
When we compare people or things, we look for similarities. When we contrast people or things, we look for differences. We usually compare and contrast at the same time.

D ▶ Role-play. Work with a partner. One of you is a famous singer, and the other is the host of a TV talk show. Write two more questions. Then act out the interview.

1. What do you like about being famous?
2. When did you start singing?
3. Who do you look up to? Who is your idol?
4. _____
5. _____

CONVERSATION STRATEGY Asking for and Giving Advice

A ▶ Practice. Complete the conversations with sentences from the box. Listen and check your answers. Then practice with a partner.

Skill Focus — Asking for and Giving Advice
We often ask for advice when we are unsure about what to do. When we give advice, we often try to put ourselves in the other person's place.

Asking for Advice
* **What should I** say to him?
* **Do you think I should** go?

Giving Advice
* **I'd** just go, **if I were in your shoes.**
* No. **I'd** tell him I had other plans.
* **Maybe you should** tell him you're sick.
* **You could always** tell him the truth.
* **You could** just go for coffee.

A: Eric asked me out tonight, but I'm exhausted. _____
_____
B: _____
A: I can't tell him that. I already told him I don't have any plans tonight. _____
B: _____
A: But I'm not sick. I don't want to lie.
B: Hmm. _____.
Just explain that you're tired.
A: But being tired doesn't sound like a good excuse. He's such a nice guy.
B: _____.
That would make it a short date.
A: Yeah. I guess a quick coffee would be OK.
B: _____

B ▶ Role-play. Work with a partner. Ask for advice about one of the situations below. Your partner should respond, using expressions and phrases from Activity A.

1. You are a good singer. Your friend wants you to join his rock band. You don't think the band is very good.
2. Your father works for a famous politician. The politician is offering you a job as his assistant. You are not really interested in politics.

Unit 1 The Other Side of Fame **7**

WRITING Mastering the Parts of a Paragraph

A ▶ Study it. Read the paragraph of opinion on page 9.

1. Find all the quantifiers in the paragraph. List them with the nouns they quantify.

QUANTIFIER AND NOUN

> **TIP Using Expressions of Quantity**
> - Use these expressions of quantity (quantifiers) with either count or non-count nouns: *no, some, a lot of, most of (the)*.
> - Use *many* and *a few* only with count nouns.
> - Use *a little* only with non-count nouns.

2. Read about the parts of a paragraph below. Then read the paragraph on page 9. Look at the colors of the lines under the sentences. Match each color with the correct part of a paragraph.

   __red__ The **topic sentence** gives the main idea of the paragraph.

   _____ **Supporting sentences** directly support the topic sentence.

   _____ **Examples** demonstrate or give details about the supporting sentences.

   _____ The **concluding sentence** restates the topic sentence.

B ▶ Write it. Write a paragraph about something you think is overrated.

1. Complete the outline below.

   Topic sentence: _____

   Supporting sentence: _____

   Example: _____

   Example: _____

   Supporting sentence: _____

   Example: _____

   Example: _____

   Concluding sentence: _____

2. Use the completed outline from Activity 1 to help you write your paragraph.

8 Unit 1 The Other Side of Fame

As I See It

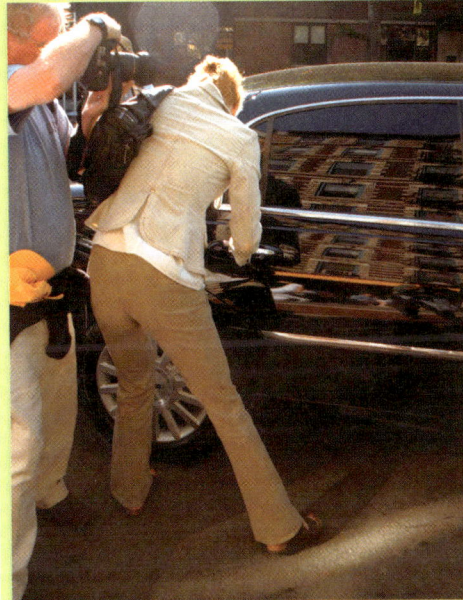

Is Fame Overrated?

Many people think it is fun to be famous, but I think fame is overrated. First of all, famous people have no privacy. Everywhere they go, people stare at them. Paparazzi take photographs of them in restaurants, stores, and even their own homes. Some crazy fans and reporters go into celebrities' mailboxes and steal their mail. Second, fame can be dangerous. Strangers sometimes try to hurt celebrities or their children. Paparazzi can be so aggressive that they cause car accidents!
5   Third, celebrities' lives involve a lot of stress. One famous celebrity said, "I have constant stress in my life. I only get a little sleep, and I'm always sick. I only want a few minutes of peace." So, while it might be fun to be famous, I think the problems of fame far outweigh the benefits.

Famous People | Fan Clubs | In the News | Email Me

Editing Checklist

- Does your paragraph have two supporting sentences?
- Does each supporting sentence have at least two examples?

PUT IT TO THE TEST

A ▶ Read.

1. Read the article. Then answer the questions that follow.

Child Stars and Fame

Lindsay Lohan hit the big time at the age of 11 with the 1998 movie *The Parent Trap*. For about eight months, she had to shuttle between the movie's sets in London and in Napa Valley, California. This raised one of the biggest issues for child stars: education. Tutors (sometimes called "set teachers") helped her keep up with her studies. But Lindsay's mom, who was also her manager, arranged for Lindsay to do most of her schooling at public schools close to home, even after she became a big star. She lived with her parents and three younger siblings on Long Island in New York. She refused several acting jobs because she did not want to live in California for months at a time. That all seems normal enough.

Still, the dangers of fame awaited her. The hit movies she made in her late teens, including *Freaky Friday* and *Mean Girls*, made her enormous amounts of money. They also made her a target of reporters and the aggressive photographers, called paparazzi, who stalk celebrities. Unfortunately, her personal life gave the press a lot to write about. Her parents, during divorce hearings, fought over Lindsay's money until a judge told them to stop. Her very wealthy father was sentenced to prison for suspicious business dealings and was repeatedly charged with assault. After moving to Los Angeles at the age of 18, Lindsay became the subject of many stories about romances and partying. Like many child stars before her, she developed an alcohol problem—before she was old enough to drink legally. The tabloid press (sensationalist newspapers) pursued her constantly. On several occasions, paparazzi who were chasing Lindsay crashed into cars she was driving.

Lindsay Lohan clearly needs a break from fame. As her mother, Dina, told CBS News, "I just pray the tabloids give us our space and leave us alone."

Sources: CBS News, "Dina Lohan: It's Hard under a Microscope." January 17, 2007. Accessed February 2007 at http://www.cbsnews.com/stories/2007/01/19/earlyshow/leisure/celebspot/main2374572.shtml?CMP=ILC-SearchStories; Ian Griggs, "A film star at 11, in rehab at 20: The Lindsay Lohan story" The Guardian, December 3, 2006. Accessed February 2007 at http://news.independent.co.uk/world/americas/article2035170.ece

2. Answer these questions about the reading.

1. Where did the Lohan family live?
   a. The Napa Valley
   b. New York
   c. London
   d. Los Angeles

2. According to the passage, paparazzi are a problem for Lindsay because
   a. they are trying to hurt her
   b. they are poor drivers
   c. they work for tabloids
   d. they constantly bother her

3. Which of the following is implied in the passage about Lindsay Lohan's father?
   a. He left the family when she was young.
   b. He stole her money.
   c. The press wrote stories about his troubles.
   d. He recently moved.

10 Unit 1 The Other Side of Fame

B ▶ Listen.

Listen to a lecture about the effects of fame. You may take notes as you listen. Then answer the question.

1. What is the lecture mainly about?
   a. Harry Potter
   b. child stars
   c. British paparazzi
   d. Daniel Radcliffe

2. Listen again to two passages from the lecture. Answer the question you hear after each passage.

   1. a. As other stars who are dating each other
      b. As members of the press
      c. As other child stars treated more harshly by the press
      d. As successful child stars

   2. a. As something that damaged Radcliffe's career
      b. As an attempt by Radcliffe to expand his career
      c. As a demonstration of Radcliffe's writing skill
      d. As one of many crimes committed by teen actors

C ▶ Personal interpretation.

Choose one of the following pictures. What is happening in the picture? How does it relate to what you have read and heard about child stars? Prepare a two-minute spoken description to present to a partner or your whole class.

D ▶ Independent writing.

Write a response of about 250 words to the following prompt. Use specific reasons and examples to support your response.

> Life as a child star can bring a mix of great rewards and big problems. In your opinion, which is more likely to be more dominant in the life of most child stars, the rewards or the problems?

2 Scents

READING AND SPEAKING

A ▶ Warm up. Work in a group.

1. Complete the chart. Write two sights, two sounds, and two smells that might indicate danger.

Sights	Sounds	Smells

2. Talk in your group. What would you do if you saw, heard, or smelled the things in the chart?

B ▶ Read. Skim the article on page 13. What is the main idea? Circle a, b, or c.
   a. Firefighters responded to an emergency call from a woman with anosmia.
   b. The fire department saved a woman in her apartment after neighbors called to report smelling gas in their building.
   c. A woman's medical condition makes her life difficult, but she's coping with the challenges she faces.

C ▶ Read again. Read the article. Then number the events in the correct sequence.
   a. _____ 911 calls were made to the fire department.
   b. _____ Firefighters forced their way into the woman's apartment.
   c. _____ Residents of the apartment complex smelled a strong odor of gas.
   d. _____ Fire crews turned off the gas at the apartment building.
   e. _____ Firefighters recommended that the woman install smoke and gas alarms.
   f. _____ The woman turned her oven on.

> **TIP** **Sequencing**
> To understand a reading, it is helpful to put events in the correct sequence—the order of what happened first, next, and so on. Look for words like *after*, *before*, and *then*, to help you.

Firefighters Respond to Gas Leak

by John Buck

Firefighters responded to reports of a strong gas **odor** coming from an apartment on Madison Avenue Saturday evening. They forced the door open and found a woman sitting in the living room. She was listening to loud music on her headphones. She didn't smell the gas that was coming from her oven because she suffers from a complete loss of her **sense** of smell—a **condition** known as anosmia.

The woman had turned on her oven to cook dinner, but the pilot light was out. Gas quickly filled the woman's apartment. Then it spread to the rest of the building. The woman didn't hear her neighbors pounding on the door because of the loud music she was playing. Neighbors called 911, and the fire department came to the scene.

After shutting off the gas supply, the fire chief talked with the woman about the incident. He recommended that she install gas detectors and smoke alarms. The woman was very embarrassed and promised to **take precautions** in the future. The fire chief turned the gas supply back on before talking with reporters about the **incident**. "She's lucky she didn't light a match," he said. "There could have been a terrible explosion."

The woman said that while anosmia is sometimes **temporary**, her condition is **permanent** as a result of a head injury. She said that she is able to **cope**, but that she **faces many challenges** due to her injury. "I live alone so I have to be very careful with food. I can't tell if it's spoiled, so I have to pay close attention to expiration dates. And last week my boyfriend told me that he liked my perfume but the **fragrance** was too strong—I used too much!"

D ▶ Pair work. Discuss these questions with a partner.
1. Think of another challenge this woman might face because of her condition. How would it be a problem? How would she cope with it?
2. What are the five senses? Which one do you think is most important or valuable? Why?
3. If you had to sacrifice one of your senses, which one would it be? Why?

LISTENING

Listen to a researcher talking about anosmia. Then check (✓) True or False for each statement.

	True	False
1. Researchers looked at medical records from the past 20 years.	☐	☐
2. People with anosmia are much more likely to have an accident than people with normal smell.	☐	☐
3. Researchers found that 74% of incidents involved cooking.	☐	☐
4. The most frequently reported accidents involved eating or drinking.	☐	☐
5. The research shows that 25% of incidents involved gas leaks.	☐	☐
6. Fewer incidents with fire were reported than with gas leaks.	☐	☐

Activating Grammar

The Simple Present, Present Continuous, Simple Past, and Past Continuous

We use simple present to talk about facts, habits, and routines.
   Natural gas **has** a strong odor.

We use the present continuous to talk about things that are happening right now, or at this general time.
   The woman **is living** with anosmia.

We use the simple past to talk about completed actions.
   Fire crews **shut off** the gas supply.

We use the past continuous to describe an action in progress at a specific time in the past.
   The neighbors **were pounding** on her door.

We also use the past continuous to describe a past action that was interrupted by a second past action. The second action that interrupts the first action is in the simple past.
   While she **was listening** to music, neighbors **called** 911.

* See page 135 for additional grammar practice.

A ▶ Read. Complete the paragraph with the correct form of the verb in parentheses. Use only the simple present, present continuous, simple past, or past continuous.

> **TIP — Verbs That Don't Take the Continuous**
> There are some verbs that you don't usually find in the continuous. These include *appear, be, forget, hate, hear, like, love, prefer, remember, see, seem, smell,* and *want*.

I was in the city last week for another job interview. Currently, I _____ (try) to get a job as a graphic designer. Anyway, while I _____ (walk) down the sidewalk I _____ (smell) a strong odor coming from a Chinese restaurant. Immediately I _____ (remember) a festival I went to in China two years ago. Many details of the festival _____ (come) rushing back to me. I felt like I was back in China. The feeling was temporary, but it made me wonder about why smells _____ (cause) the brain to produce such strong memories. I _____ (have) another similar incident recently. One day I _____ (talk) to a female interviewer. She _____ (wear) a perfume I didn't know the name of, but suddenly all I could think about was my grandmother. My grandmother _____ (die) many years ago, but I could see her face and felt very close to her. The interviewer was wearing my grandmother's perfume!

14 Unit 2 Scents

B ▶ Interview. Interview a partner. Ask and answer questions about scents using the simple present, present continuous, simple past, and past continuous. Use the questions listed below or think of your own.

1. Do you wear perfume or cologne?
2. What is your favorite scent or fragrance? What is your least favorite odor?
3. Are there any fragrances or odors that you associate with specific memories? Explain.

VOCABULARY

A ▶ Practice. Match the words on the left with their meanings on the right.

1. ___ fragrance
2. ___ condition
3. ___ temporary
4. ___ permanent
5. ___ face challenges
6. ___ senses
7. ___ incident
8. ___ take precautions
9. ___ cope
10. ___ odor

a. deal with difficulties
b. smell or scent, sometimes unpleasant
c. occurrence or event
d. prepare for risk or danger
e. lasting for an unlimited time
f. smell or scent, usually pleasant
g. physical state
h. survive or manage
i. sight, hearing, taste, touch, smell
j. lasting for a limited time

B ▶ Listen. Listen to information about people and things. Then complete the sentences with the vocabulary words from Activity A. Use each word once.

1. Carlos's medical _____ is _____. He'll feel better soon.
2. Public restrooms can have a bad _____. There should always be an air freshener with a nice _____.
3. There was a dangerous _____ in my neighborhood. Now we have to _____.
4. Just about everybody has to _____ in life. But some people are able to _____ better than others.
5. With the _____ loss of one of her _____ she can no longer enjoy flowers in the same way.

LISTENING Perfume School

A ▶ Discuss. What do you think this person is doing? What senses is she using?

B ▶ Listen. Check (✓) the sentence that gives the gist of the news report. Why is this choice correct? Why are the other choices incorrect?

1. ___ Provence is an area of southern France that has many aromatic plants and is important for the perfume industry.

2. ___ Four teenagers were selected to attend a perfume workshop in France, and most of them had a positive experience.

3. ___ Padma didn't enjoy the perfume workshop as much as the other teens, but she did think Provence was beautiful.

> **Skill Focus** **Listening for Gist**
> The gist of a lecture, report, or conversation is similar to the main idea of a reading. It's the most important idea. To check your understanding of the gist of a listening passage, try to identify several details that support it.

C ▶ Listen again. Did each student enjoy the experience? Circle *yes* or *no*. Then write something each student said that supports your answer.

Student	Did they enjoy the experience?
1. Kyle	yes no
2. Padma	yes no
3. Pedro	yes no
4. Lin	yes no

16 Unit 2 Scents

D ▶ Group work. Ask and answer these questions.

1. Would you be interested in attending a perfume school? Why or why not?
2. Do you burn incense or have other scents in your home? Explain.
3. Do you use fragrances in other places? (For example, in the car, in a clothes drawer, or in the bathroom) Think of other examples, and explain why you use fragrances in these places.
4. Do you usually smell your food before you eat it? Why?
5. How else are scents important in your life?

CONVERSATION STRATEGY   Asking for Additional Information

A ▶ Listen and practice. Complete the conversation with phrases from the box. Listen and check your answers. Then practice the conversation with a partner.

* Could you explain. . . ?
* I'd like to know if. . . .
* Tell me more about. . . .
* Is there anything else. . . ?

A: We'll have a new product ready for the market soon. Pet perfumes!

B: _____ this. It's something I might be interested in.

A: Well, the idea came from a survey of our pet food customers. They wanted their pets to smell better.

B: I'd like my dog to smell better when he comes in the house. But I don't think I'd want him to smell like flowers.

A: Right. Most pet owners prefer a fresh, simple smell.

B: Hmm. _____ what *fresh* means, exactly?

A: Well, according to our survey, "fresh" smells like the outdoors, or a light soap.

B: Oh. That's interesting. _____ you'd like to tell me about these perfumes?

A: The names! Our cat fragrance is Meow and the fragrance for dogs is Woof.

B: _____ these perfumes are available to order now.

B ▶ Role-play. Work with a partner. Take turns presenting information and using phrases from Activity A to ask for additional information. Use these ideas or choose your own.

1. Talk about your next vacation/trip.
2. Talk about your job/company.
3. Talk about your family/relationships.
4. Talk about your plans for the future.

WRITING   Writing Topic Sentences

> **Skill Focus**
>
> **Strong Topic Sentences**
> A paragraph is a group of sentences about one topic. The topic can be a group of things (for example, flowers), an abstract thing (for example, peace), or something that has several parts or details (for example, the library). A topic sentence says something specific about the topic; it gives a main, or controlling, idea about the topic.

A ▶ Study it. Look at the reading on page 19.

1. Read the first paragraph.

The topic is "the scent of pine." Notice how the writer says something specific about the topic in the topic sentence. Notice how the topic sentence *controls* the topic of the paragraph; all of the other sentences in the paragraph support it.

Strong topic sentence:
I like to use the scent of pine in my home.

Compare the good topic sentence above with the other sentences below. These would *not* be good topic sentences for the paragraph. They are too general. They don't contain a specific, main, or controlling idea.

Weak topic sentences:
The scent of pine is nice.
I enjoy the scent of pine.

2. Read the second paragraph, and check (✓) the best topic sentence from the list below. Then write it on the line at the beginning of the paragraph.

___ There are many ways to get rid of unpleasant odors.

___ Baking soda is a great product.

___ Baking soda can be used to reduce unpleasant, everyday odors.

3. Read the third paragraph, and write a good topic sentence at the beginning of the paragraph.

B ▶ Write it.

Write a paragraph about how people can smell good all day. You can include information about things you can do with your hair, your skin, or your clothes. You can include tips for fresh breath. You can also talk about avoiding things that make you smell bad. Whatever you choose, be sure you have a topic sentence that contains a specific, controlling main idea.

Common Sense and Home Scents

I like to use the scent of pine in my home. To keep my kitchen smelling fresh, I use a pine-scented dish detergent and a pine-scented cleaner for my kitchen counters. I keep a candle that has a strong pine
5 fragrance in the bathroom. It gives the bathroom a clean feeling. I also use a spray air freshener that has a light pine scent in all the rooms of my home. I love the smell of the pines woods near my house, so I try to create that smell indoors, too.

10 Baking soda can be used in a cat's litter box to help to get rid of odor. Just mix it in with the litter. You can also keep an open box of baking soda in your refrigerator to cut down on strong odors from various foods. A box will last about three months. You can also use baking soda as a powder cleanser for sinks and drains, and it will eliminate odors from these areas and keep them smelling fresh. You can even sprinkle baking soda in foul-smelling sports shoes and notice some improvement. It might not
15 save you from a skunk, but for many common odor problems, baking soda is a good solution.

One thing you can do is use a lightly scented laundry detergent. This will give your clothes a pleasant smell. You can also hang your clothes out in the sun to dry, rather than using a dryer. Nothing will make clothes
20 smell better than fresh air and sunshine. Another option is to keep sachets—small scented packets—in your clothes drawers and closets. It's not that hard to have great-smelling things to wear!

Editing Checklist

- Did you write about a single topic?
- Does your topic sentence say something specific? Does it give a main or controlling idea about the topic?
- Do all of the sentences in your paragraph support your topic sentence?
- Do you have a concluding sentence that restates your topic sentence?

PUT IT TO THE TEST

A ▶ Read.

1. Read the article, and then answer the questions on the next page.

Advertising for Your Nose

Imagine this: You are waiting at a bus stop when you begin to smell the scent of chocolate chip cookies baking nearby. Is it your imagination? Is there a bakery nearby? If you were in San Francisco, you were not imagining it.
5 The California Milk Processor Board tried a new marketing technique: scented bus shelter advertisements. The marketing team infused five bus shelters with the smell of fresh-baked cookies. The theory behind the campaign is that a scent can be memorable. They wanted to
10 encourage people to buy milk with their cookies.

The marketing campaign was **temporary**, however. City officials in San Francisco ordered the removal of the cookie scent from the public bus shelters. Critics of the idea were saying that the smell would be offensive to
15 people who have chemical sensitivities and the aroma would trigger adverse reactions, such as headaches, nausea, and **incidents** of seizures and asthma attacks. They were also concerned that homeless people and others who cannot afford to buy cookies were being
20 forced to sniff the scent while they were waiting for the bus. People in favor of the advertising campaign said that they would rather sniff chocolate chip cookies than typical city smells such as exhaust fumes, dirt, and other less desirable odors.

25 Olfactory marketing (relating a scent to a product) is not new. Auto dealerships often pipe in a "new car" smell in their buildings. Convenience stores have fresh-brewed coffee, flower shops are often infused with floral fragrances, and moviegoers are enticed by
30 the smell of fresh popcorn. This was the first time olfactory marketing was done in a bus shelter in the United States but it has been tried in London before. One company infused bus shelters with a citrus scent to advertise a new fruit drink.

Sources: CBS News, "Smells Like Cookies at the Bus Stop." December 5, 2006; Accessed February 2007 at http://www.cbsnews.com/stories/2006/12/05/tech/ printable2228159.shtml; Rachel Gordon, "Cookie scent in bus shelters makes for heated debate," San Francisco Chronicle, December 2, 2006; Accessed February 2007 at http://www.sfgate.com/cgi-bin/article.cgi?file=/c/a/2006/12/02/BAGE2MO35E1.DTL; Rachel Gordon, "Freshly baked ads are toast: City orders that cookie-scented strips in bus shelters be removed," San Francisco Chronicle, December 5, 2006; Accessed February 2007 at http://sfgate.com/cgi-bin/article.cgi?f=/c/a/2006/12/05/BAGQDMPQB319.DTL

2. Answer these questions about the reading.

1. All of the following are mentioned in the passage as being true about the cookie scent EXCEPT that _____.
   a. few people had asthma attacks from smelling it
   b. it was removed from the bus shelters
   c. critics suggested that it was offensive to people with chemical sensitivities
   d. an advertising company in London infused a citrus smell in bus shelters

2. The word **temporary** in the passage is closest in meaning to _____.
   a. not popular
   b. effective
   c. lasted for a short time
   d. permanent

3. The word **incidents** in the passage is closest in meaning to _____.
   a. problems
   b. sickness
   c. times
   d. occurrences

20 Unit 2 Scents

B ▶ Listen.

Listen to a conversation between an advertising representative and an owner of several bakeries. You may take notes as you listen. Then answer the question.

1. Why does the woman visit the man's business?
   a. To hear his ideas about how to market his new bakeries around town
   b. To buy bread
   c. To describe some proposals for marketing his business
   d. To get a job

2. Listen again to two parts of the conversation, and answer the question after each part.

   1. a. He likes the ideas but he is not sure they are going to sell his products.
      b. He doesn't think they are going to work.
      c. He likes the ideas and wants to pursue them.
      d. He doesn't believe in the power of scents in advertising.

   2. a. She doesn't think the results from the field research are very convincing.
      b. She doesn't believe in the idea of using smell to sell.
      c. She believes in the effectiveness of olfactory marketing.
      d. She uses olfactory marketing all of the time.

C ▶ Personal interpretation.

Look at the comic strip below. What is happening in the picture? How does it relate to what you have read and heard about a smell bringing back memories? Are there any scents that you associate with a particular person, place, or situation? Prepare a two-minute spoken description about a familiar scent and the memory you associate with that smell.

D ▶ Independent speaking.

Set a timer for 45 seconds, or have a classmate time you. Within that short time, give a spoken response to the following prompt. You will have 15 seconds to prepare your response. Do not write out or memorize it in advance.

> City officials in San Francisco ordered that the cookie-scented strips be removed from the public bus shelters. Do you agree or disagree with the decision? Give specific reasons for your opinion.

3 Relating

READING AND SPEAKING

A ▶ Warm up. Look at the photo, the title of the article, and the headings on page 23. Check (✓) the sentence that you think best describes the relationship between the boy and the gorilla.

   a. ___ The child is helping the gorilla train to be a mother.

   b. ___ The gorilla stole the child.

   c. ___ The gorilla is helping the child.

B ▶ Read. Read the article and answer the questions.

1. Was the sentence you chose in Activity A correct?
2. Write the letter of each heading next to the information found under that heading in the article. Put an "X" next to information that is not in the article.
    a. A normal day turns into a nightmare
    b. Binti to the rescue
    c. Why did Binti help?

   1. ___ Binti had training to become a mother.
   2. ___ The boy's mother tried to rescue her son from the top of the fence.
   3. ___ Binti picked up the boy and put him near the door.
   4. ___ The boy fell from a dangerous height into the gorilla area.

C ▶ Read again. Check (✓) the inference you can make based on each sentence.

1. The boy didn't move.
    a. ___ The boy was afraid of the gorillas.
    b. ___ The boy had an injury.
2. In seconds, his mother's expression changed from frustrated to horrified.
    a. ___ Even before he fell, the boy's behavior was upsetting his mother.
    b. ___ The mother didn't mind the boy climbing the fence.
3. Binti was a good-natured gorilla with her own baby.
    a. ___ Binti didn't like other gorillas.
    b. ___ Binti might be good-natured with human children.

Skill Focus: Making Inferences
When you make an inference about a reading, you fill in information the writer does not give you directly by making a guess based on the information that the writer does give you.

4. Placing the doll in front of the door is a part of the training. Perhaps Binti simply remembered doing this in her training.
    a. ___ Binti thought the boy was a doll.
    b. ___ Binti wanted to play.

22   Unit 3   Relating

A Mother's Love?

A normal day turns into a nightmare

In 1996, a woman and her son visited the Chicago Zoo. They stopped to look at the gorillas. Suddenly, the three-year-old boy climbed to the top of a fence around the gorilla area. He tried to stand on the fence, but he fell into the gorilla area 24 feet below. He didn't move. In seconds, his mother's expression changed from frustrated to horrified. The zookeepers stopped talking to the visitors and ran to the entrance of the gorilla area.

Binti to the rescue

The zookeepers knew the boy was in real danger. Gorillas live in groups, but they can be **antisocial** if a stranger enters their group. Some of them can also be **aggressive**. Biting was a serious possibility. The keepers needed to get the boy out. Then an **amazing** thing happened. A female gorilla named Binti showed her **compassionate** side. She picked up the boy and held him. He still wasn't moving. The keepers were hopeful. Binti was a **good-natured** gorilla with her own baby. She was very **patient**. Binti carried the boy to the door of the cage and gently laid him down. An ambulance arrived on the scene. Paramedics took the boy to the hospital. It was an **exhausting day** for the boy and his mother, but the boy fully recovered.

Why did Binti help?

Writer Stephen Budiansky interviewed several scientists about Binti for his book, *If a Lion Could Talk*. Many people believe Binti understood that the boy needed her help. Only gorillas in the wild naturally care for their young. Gorillas in zoos need to learn to become mothers. Keepers teach them to hold dolls **gently**. Placing the doll near the cage door is a part of the training. Perhaps Binti remembered doing this in her training. It's a possibility many researchers are interested in testing.

D ▶ **Pair work.** Discuss these questions with a partner.
1. Do you believe Binti understood her actions and wanted to help the child?
2. Do you think animals and humans can have meaningful relationships? Explain.

LISTENING

Listen and number the sentences in the correct sequence.

a. _____ The boy climbed the fence and fell into the gorilla area.
b. _____ The zookeepers got the boy out of the gorilla area.
c. _____ Binti the gorilla picked up the boy and put him in front of the door.
d. _____ The zookeepers rushed to the door.
e. _____ A boy and his mother were looking at the gorillas.

ACTIVATING GRAMMAR

Gerunds and Infinitives

Some verbs can take either gerunds or infinitives as objects.
> They loved **visiting** the zoo.
> They loved **to visit** the zoo.

The verbs *stop, remember,* and *forget,* can be followed by either a gerund or an infinitive, but the meaning will be different.
> They stopped **to look** at the gorillas.   First they were walking, and then they stopped and looked.
> They stopped **looking** at the gorillas.   First they were looking, but then they stopped.

* See page 135 for additional grammar practice.

A ▶ Read. Read the paragraph. Find sentences with errors involving gerunds or infinitives. Rewrite the sentences correctly on the lines below.

Before dying in 1997, Glynn Wolfe had many meaningful relationships with women—an amazing 29 of them resulted in marriage, and 28 of those ended in divorce. (He didn't remember to marry
5   number 25. And he always forgot her name.)

For some reason, Glynn never stopped to try for a successful marriage. He even married two women twice. He never stopped thinking about the chances of a marriage ending in divorce. He always believed it might work out.
10   Unfortunately for Glynn, he was never able to find success in marriage. Toward the end of his life, a British TV company arranged his last wedding for a TV program. Then he and his 29th wife, Linda Essex, spent a week together before he died. His last wife says, "I will never
15   forget to spend time with him. He was very good-natured." But not everyone thought Glynn was patient. His son says, "He divorced one wife for eating sunflower seeds in bed." Perhaps she forgot offering him some!

1. _____
2. _____
3. _____
4. _____
5. _____

🎧 **B ▶ Listen.** Listen to each situation. Check (✓) the sentence if it is a good response.

1. ___ I know! They rush into the next marriage and make the same mistakes.
2. ___ Oh. Then I'll have someone else pick him up at the airport.
3. ___ Your sister is so good-natured. I'm sure she doesn't mind that you forgot her birthday.
4. ___ Good. She's patient, but she hates it when people miss appointments.
5. ___ Did you ever ask her about it? Maybe she was just a nervous person.

24   Unit 3   Relating

VOCABULARY

A ▶ Practice. Read the questionnaire. Write the adjective described in each question.

| aggressive | antisocial | exhausting | gentle | patient |
| amazing | compassionate | frustrated | good-natured | |

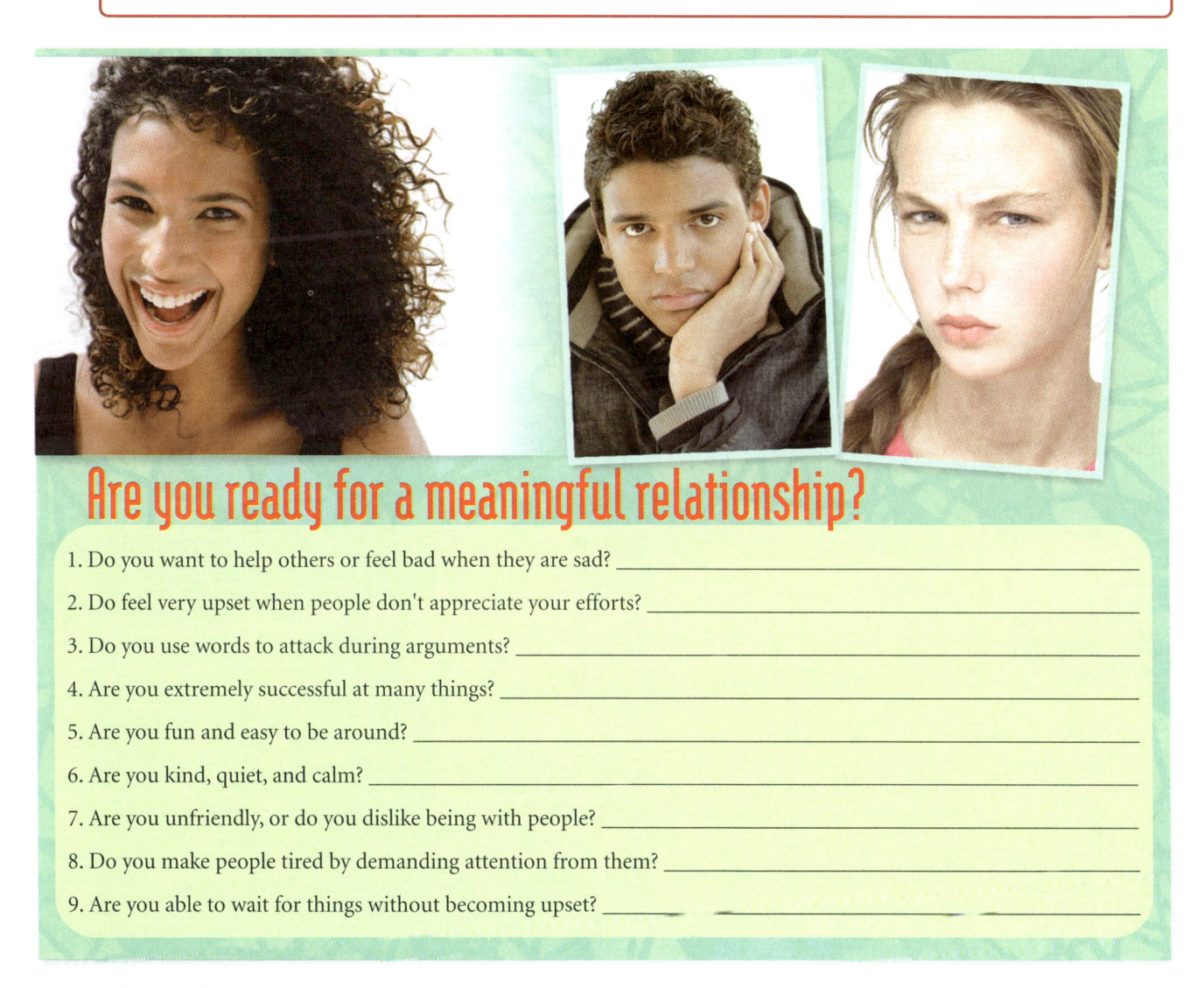

Are you ready for a meaningful relationship?

1. Do you want to help others or feel bad when they are sad? _____
2. Do feel very upset when people don't appreciate your efforts? _____
3. Do you use words to attack during arguments? _____
4. Are you extremely successful at many things? _____
5. Are you fun and easy to be around? _____
6. Are you kind, quiet, and calm? _____
7. Are you unfriendly, or do you dislike being with people? _____
8. Do you make people tired by demanding attention from them? _____
9. Are you able to wait for things without becoming upset? _____

B ▶ Pair work. Work with a partner.

1. Complete the chart with the adjectives from above.

Positive qualities	Negative qualities	Could be positive or negative

2. Work with a partner. Ask and answer the questions in Activity A. Give examples and explanations for your answers.

LISTENING Resolving Conflict

A ▶ Discuss. Read the poster below.
1. What is your first impression of Dr. Prince? Circle the letter of one adjective.
   a. compassionate   b. aggressive   c. gentle   d. antisocial
2. Work with a partner. Discuss how the picture and text helped form your impression.

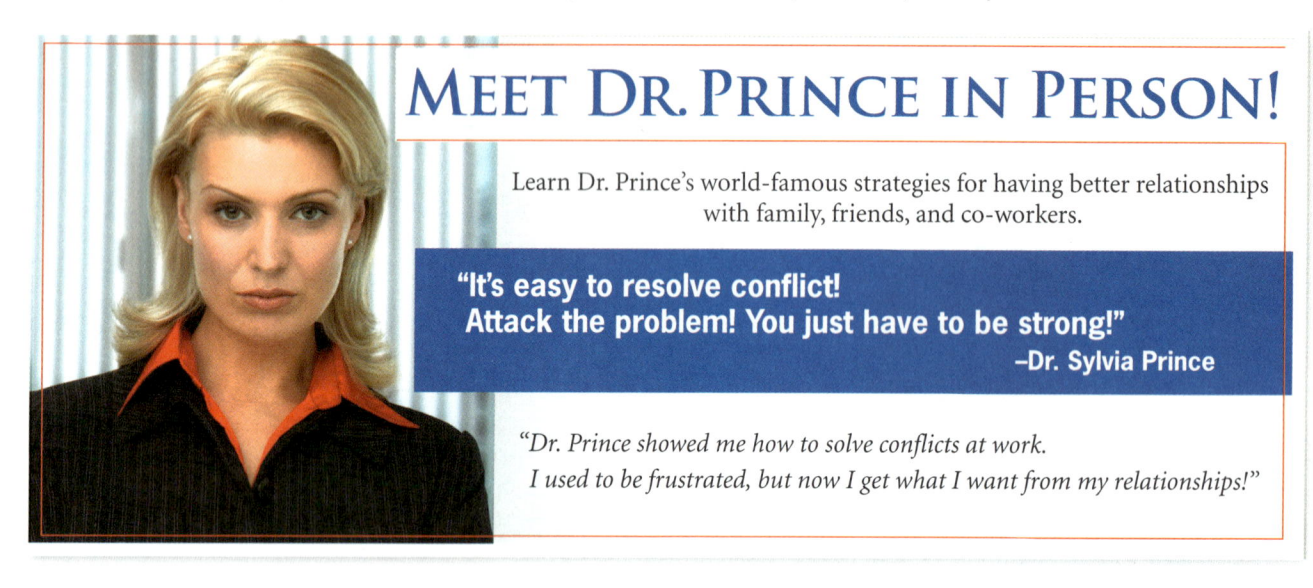

MEET DR. PRINCE IN PERSON!

Learn Dr. Prince's world-famous strategies for having better relationships with family, friends, and co-workers.

"It's easy to resolve conflict! Attack the problem! You just have to be strong!"
—Dr. Sylvia Prince

"Dr. Prince showed me how to solve conflicts at work. I used to be frustrated, but now I get what I want from my relationships!"

B ▶ Listen. Check (✓) the sentences Dr. Prince agrees with.

1. _____ Most people know something about resolving conflict.
2. _____ Listening to people complain about their relationships is exhausting.
3. _____ Compassionate people can't resolve conflict.
4. _____ Being patient is important.
5. _____ Be honest and gentle about your reasons for being unhappy in a relationship.
6. _____ If things don't improve, leave the relationship.

Which checked sentences confirm your first impression? Which are surprises?

C ▶ Listen again. Before you listen, predict Dr. Prince's responses to the two audience questions you heard her repeat. Then listen to her responses and check your answers.

Skill Focus: Using Prior Knowledge and Impressions to Make Predictions
We combine our impression about a person with information we have about them to predict their opinions or responses.

Question 1: ... Should I break up with her?
   Dr. Prince:
   a. Break up immediately.
   b. Be patient. Do nothing now.
   c. No. Move to New York.

Question 2: ... What do you think?
   Dr. Prince:
   a. Look for a very good job in LA.
   b. Get out of the relationship immediately.
   c. Be patient. If he doesn't change his mind in a couple months, end the relationship.

Unit 3 Relating

D ▶ Group work. Read and discuss the situation below. What advice would Dr. Prince give Dina? What advice would she give Anna? What advice would you offer?

Anna just started dating Dina's ex-boyfriend, David. Dina wants to continue to be friends with Anna, but she doesn't want to see Anna with David, and she doesn't want Anna to talk about him. Dina wants everyone to continue to be friends. She doesn't want to worry about making sure Anna and David don't see each other. She also thinks she should be able to talk to Anna about David.

CONVERSATION STRATEGY Commiserating

A ▶ Pair work. Complete the conversations with sentences from the box. Listen and check your answers. Then practice the conversations with a partner.

> * **How could she do that to you?** You must feel terrible.
> * **The same thing happened to me.** I asked him for help.
> * **That must be hard on you.** But he's been your friend for years.
> * **Tell me about it.** I'm really frustrated in that class.
> * **I'm really sorry to hear that.** But people will realize she lied. Forget about it.

1. **A:** I got a terrible e-mail from Vincent. He doesn't want to be my friend anymore.
   B: _____. I'm sure he'll change his mind.

2. **A:** My roommate was talking behind my back. She told all sorts of lies about me.
   B: _____.
   A: I do! And some people believe the lies. They won't talk to me. I can't sleep.
   B: _____.

3. **A:** Mr. Banks isn't patient this semester. He was my favorite teacher last semester.
   B: Hah! _____. I don't understand anything he says.
   A: And I went to him after class to say I didn't understand the lesson. He didn't have time to talk to me.
   B: _____. But he was too busy.

B ▶ Role-play. Work with a partner. Role-play the situations below. One of you is the person described. The other commiserates.

1. Your brother has driven your car without your permission. He was in an accident.
2. You have a very sick parent in the hospital.
3. You are angry at your best friend for _____.

Unit 3 Relating **27**

WRITING Using Graphic Organizers for Planning

A ▶ Study it. Read the paragraph on page 29.

1. The paragraph tells about three phases in a relationship. The phases are listed at the top of the chart below. Find the places in the paragraph where the phases change, and use a slash (/) to mark the places.

2. Complete the chart with the details and examples from each section of the paragraph.

> **Skill Focus: Using Graphic Organizers for Planning**
> It is important to organize your thoughts before you write. Organizers such as mind maps, question and answer lists, and charts are very useful. You may prefer using one type of organizer, or you may like using different types of organizers for different types of writing.

Past relationship characteristics	Why/How relationship changed	Current relationship characteristics
bad relationship argued about wearing _____	went to college met _____ learned about _____, _____, _____, didn't care about _____	close relationship talk _____ stopped _____ go _____ read _____
Example 1: party had to _____, _____ went without makeup, felt _____	Example: went to a party, forgot to _____, felt _____	Example: mother helped me through _____ when _____
Example 2: She always _____ my phone calls		

28 Unit 3 Relating

Growing Up and Growing Closer

My relationship with my mother changed after I went to college. When I was at home, we argued about many things, for example, wearing makeup and talking on the phone. One time, before a big party, she refused to let me leave the house.
5 She thought my makeup was too heavy. I had to wash my face before I went to the party. I was the only girl without makeup, and I was so angry. And my mom always yelled at me if I talked on the phone too long. Sometimes she yelled so loudly to tell me to hang up that the person I was talking
10 to could hear her. I couldn't stand her.

But after a few weeks at college, I changed. I met new people. I started learning about history, politics, and the world. I didn't have the time or patience for long phone conversations. I stopped caring so much about things like makeup. One
15 time I went to a party with no makeup on, but I felt fine. I just laughed about it. My new ways of thinking brought me closer to my mother. Now, I talk to my mother every day. We stopped arguing. We go to movies together and read the same books. I tell her about my problems and she gives me
20 good advice. Last month, my mother helped me through a bad time when I broke up with my boyfriend. My mother is an amazing person. I know that now.

B ▶ Write it. Write a paragraph about a relationship in your life that changed over time.

Use the chart to organize your thoughts before you write your paragraph.

Past relationship characteristics	Why/How relationship changed	Current relationship characteristics
Example:	Example:	Example:

Editing Checklist

- Have you presented three phases of the relationship clearly?
- Have you included all the important information from your chart in your paragraph?
- Have you checked for grammatical or vocabulary errors?

PUT IT TO THE TEST

A ▶ Read.

1. Read the article. Then answer the questions that follow.

Outsourcing Mom and Dad

Sarah Cunningham had a hard time getting her baby to stop crying. She had tried everything: rocking, carrying him, and turning on the vacuum cleaner. Finally she contacted Fussy Baby Support Services. After two hours of observation, the representatives concluded that the baby was overstimulated and needed a more soothing environment. They taught Sarah how to make her home more relaxing and she immediately saw results.

At times, being a parent can be frustrating and many affluent parents are looking for assistance. According to one parent-help service in New York City, there has been a 50% increase in parents coming in for help with parental challenges. Some parents are willing to pay $60 an hour to have someone toilet train their child, get their daughter to agree on modest school clothes, teach their son how to organize his bedroom, teach their kid to ride a bike, manage their kids' homework each week, and even sit up all night in their child's room in case they have a nightmare.

There are many reasons affluent parents hire someone to help their children. Impatience and lack of confidence are typical reasons for outsourcing parental duties. Also, excellence is often expected in these families and therefore parents hire an expert. These parents also want to avoid the exasperating confrontations of childrearing. They don't want to get frustrated and ruin the relationship they have with their children. Child psychologists however, believe that when parents are not present for major steps in their children's lives, they are destroying their relationship with their children. The bond between a parent and a child can only be built through quality time spent with one another. Children need and want to spend time with their parents. Children learn more about life through their parents' examples than anything else in their lives.

Sources: Betsy Hart, "Some Parental Duties Just Shouldn't be Outsourced," Jewish World Review, April 5, 2005. Accessed March 2007 at http://www.jewishworldreview.com/cols/ hart040505.asp; Hillary Stout, "Parents Outsource Potty-Training," Startup Journal, April 4, 2005. Accessed March 2007 at http://startup.wsj.com/ideas/ services/20050404-stout.htm

2. Answer these questions about the reading.

1. Why does the author mention the viewpoint of child psychologists?
   a. To show how outsourcing affects children
   b. To criticize parents
   c. To praise parents
   d. To support the parents' decision to outsource

2. The author discusses "quality time" in order to _____.
   a. explain the reasons for outsourcing
   b. highlight a negative aspect of outsourcing
   c. point out an advantage of outsourcing
   d. criticize parents who outsource

3. The word they in the passage refers to _____.
   a. the children
   b. the psychologists
   c. the child and the parents
   d. the parents

Unit 3 Relating

B ▶ Listen.

Listen to a lecture about parent-child relationships. You may take notes as you listen. Then answer the questions.

1. According to the lecturer, what happens when a child wants to just talk about something and a parent gives advice?
    a. The child accepts the advice.
    b. The child stops talking.
    c. The child tells more of the story.
    d. The child is happy to have their help.

2. What is "reflective listening?"
    a. Acknowledging someone's words, mood, and emotions
    b. Mimicking everything the person says
    c. Giving someone a solution to a problem
    d. Talking to someone

3. What can be inferred from the lecture about what kids really want from their parents?
    a. Kids don't want to be told what to do.
    b. Kids just want to be left alone.
    c. Kids want their parents' attention.
    d. Kids want their parents' advice.

C ▶ Personal interpretation.

How do you feel about parents who outsource parental duties and activities? Would it be appropriate for the parent to hire someone to help them with certain activities? Which ones? Why? Prepare a two-minute spoken response to these questions.

D ▶ Integrated writing.

Write a response of about 150 words to the following prompt. You have 20 minutes to plan and write your response.

> Summarize the points made in the lecture, being sure to specifically explain how they strengthen points made in the reading passage.

Unit 3 Relating 31

4 Digging

READING AND SPEAKING

A ▶ Warm up. How are these photos related to the unit title, "Digging"? What else do people dig for, either physically or intellectually? Write three things.

1. _____
2. _____
3. _____

B ▶ Read. Skim the article and check (✓) the main idea.

1. ___ A woman was injured while she was working in a mine in Africa looking for a large diamond called the Lesotho Promise.
2. ___ A woman discovered the Lesotho Promise while working in a mine in Lesotho.
3. ___ A miner screamed with excitement when she realized she was going to be rich after discovering a valuable diamond.

C ▶ Read again. Read the article again, and write what these words refer to.

1. *some* (paragraph 1, line [2]) _____
2. *It* (paragraph 1, line [3]) _____
3. *They* (paragraph 2, line [11]) _____
4. *It* (paragraph 3, line [12]) _____
5. *They* (paragraph 4, line [17]) _____

> **Skill Focus: Understanding What Pronouns Refer To**
>
> In reading a text, it's important to understand what words like *he, she, it, they, their, these,* and *those* refer to. Usually, these words replace ones found in the preceding sentences.

D ▶ Pair work. Work with a partner. Ask and answer the questions.

1. In addition to mining, what occupations involve digging in the earth?
2. What kinds of occupations involve digging into a person's background?
3. What kinds of occupations involve digging up other information?
4. Do you think you would be well-suited to any of these jobs? Why or why not?

The Lesotho Promise Diamond

A woman was sorting through rocks at the Letseng Diamond Mine when suddenly she screamed. When people heard her, some thought that she had been injured. Some thought that she had been electrocuted. In fact, the screaming had nothing to do with an injury. It was due to sheer excitement. The woman had just discovered a perfect white diamond, and it was the size of a golf ball.

The huge African gem, now known as the Lesotho Promise, is not the biggest diamond ever discovered. The largest diamond ever found was the South African Cullinan, discovered in 1905. It was an astonishing 3,106 carats. (One carat is equal to 0.2 grams.) The 777 carat Millennium Star was unearthed in the Democratic Republic of Congo in 1993. But the Lesotho Promise is the biggest diamond discovered so far in this century. **Gemologists** say that, uncut, it's 603 carats. They also say it is of the very best color quality.

The Lesotho Promise sold at an auction in Belgium for more than $12 million. It was purchased by the South African Diamond Corporation, which owns the luxury jeweler, Graff.

Very little is known about the woman who found the diamond. The Letseng Mine is located high in the mountains of Lesotho. Lesotho is a tiny mountain country completely surrounded by South Africa. Most of the world's diamonds come from Africa. Mine workers are generally poor. They don't share in the profits from their findings.

LISTENING

Listen to the sentences and check (✓) True or False for each sentence.

	True	False
1.	☐	☐
2.	☐	☐
3.	☐	☐
4.	☐	☐
5.	☐	☐
6.	☐	☐

ACTIVATING GRAMMAR

Dependent and Independent Clauses

An independent clause contains a subject and a verb and expresses a complete thought. It is a complete sentence and can stand alone. A dependent clause contains a subject and a verb, but does not express a complete thought. It is not a complete sentence, and it cannot stand alone.

Dependent clauses often start with *after, although, as, if, because, before, even if, in order to, since, though, unless, until, when,* or *while.*

The woman made the discovery **while she was sorting through rocks.**
  independent clause   dependent clause

A comma is used after a dependent clause if it starts a sentence.

When the woman screamed, some people thought she had been injured.
   dependent clause   independent clause

If two independent clauses are joined by connecting words *and, but,* or *so* to form one sentence, a comma comes before the connecting word.

She had just discovered a perfect white diamond, **and** it was the size of a golf ball.
       independent clause   independent clause

* See page 135 for additional grammar practice.

A ▶ Read. Read the paragraph. Write DC (dependent clause) or IC (independent clause) under each underlined clause.

Digging for Truffles

Digging for truffles is serious business. Because they cannot be cultivated and are difficult to find,
1._____   2._____
truffles are very expensive. Black truffles sell for hundreds of dollars, and white truffles can bring in over a thousand
3._____   4._____   5._____
dollars each. Truffles often reappear in the same area year after year, so hunters attempt to keep the locations of their
              6._____   7._____
findings secret. They often work at night, wearing dark clothing, so that others won't see them. Many use dogs in their
                8._____   9._____   10._____
work, although pigs have also traditionally been used in truffle-hunting. Either animal can smell truffles lying up to a
        11._____   12._____
foot beneath the surface of the ground.

When a dog or pig finds a truffle, the hunter digs it
      13._____   14._____
up using a tool called a sapin. The truffles are quickly
                             15._____
sold to chefs and owners of the finest restaurants.

Gastronomists (food experts) judge truffles as much by
16._____
their smell as by their flavor. To maximize the smell,
                              17._____
truffles are usually served raw.
18._____

34 Unit 4 Digging

B ▶ Pair work. Complete these sentences with an independent or dependent clause. Then talk to a partner about what you wrote.

1. I'm always happy _____
2. _____ in order to succeed.
3. Before I die, _____
4. _____ I get very excited.
5. Because of my parents, _____

VOCABULARY

A ▶ Listen. Listen to this career counselor talking about possible jobs. Check (✓) the *-ist* nouns that you hear.

> **TIP** **Vocabulary**
> You can often find the suffix *-ist* added to a noun to form an occupation word.
> **Example:** A person who plays the piano is a *pianist*.

1. artist _____
2. chemist _____
3. receptionist _____
4. cyclist _____
5. environmentalist _____
6. columnist _____
7. geologist _____
8. linguist _____
9. psychiatrist _____
10. violinist _____
11. cartoonist _____
12. economist _____

B ▶ Pair work. Work with a partner. Write nouns ending in the suffix *-ist* in the left column of the chart. Use words from Activity A, or use different words. Then talk about what people in these occupations do, and complete the right column.

Nouns Ending in *-ist*	Does or Believes

LISTENING A Solid Foundation

A ▶ Pair work. Work with a partner. Look at the pictures. For each situation, write topics you think you will hear the people discuss. Also, write any words and phrases you think you might hear.

1. Possible topics: _____

   Possible words and phrases: _____

2. Possible topics: _____

   Possible words and phrases: _____

B ▶ Listen.

1. As you listen, look at your answers in Activity A. Did you hear any of the words or phrases you expected to hear?
2. Write the topic of each situation. Did you come close to guessing it?

   Topic 1: _____

   Topic 2: _____

C ▶ Listen again. Before you listen again, try to answer the questions below about each situation—although you probably didn't understand, and don't remember, every word. Then listen and check your answers.

> **Skill Focus**
> **Getting Basic Information without Understanding Every Word**
> In addition to the gist, you can often understand other basic information in a conversation without catching every word.

Situation 1

1. Why doesn't the woman remember much about her father? _____
2. What does the woman want to talk about? _____
3. How does the psychiatrist respond? _____

Situation 2

1. What does the police officer think the suspect did? _____
2. When does the police officer say the crime happened? _____
3. Who does the suspect say can prove that he's innocent? _____

36 Unit 4 Digging

D ▶ Group work.

1. Work in a group. Compare your answers from Activity A.
2. Recreate the conversation for one of the situations. Try to use words and phrases from the recording. Fill in what you didn't catch, or don't remember, with your own words.
3. Choose two people from your group to read your conversation to the class.

CONVERSATION STRATEGY   Correcting a Misinterpretation

A ▶ Pair work.
Complete the conversation between a psychiatrist and a patient using sentences from the box. Listen and check your answers. Then practice the conversation with a partner.

> * **Actually, what I mean is that** *I'm* not able to talk about certain things.
> * **I guess I'm not expressing myself very well.** My mother wouldn't be angry.
> * No, **that's not really what I meant to say.** Our relationship is basically good.
> * No, **that's not what I mean.**
> * **What I'm trying to say is** that the problem isn't with my mother.

Skill Focus — Correcting a Misinterpretation
Sometimes a listener will misinterpret your words. It's important to know how to correct the listener politely.

A: So, based on what you've said, you don't have a very good relationship with your mother.

B: _____ But there are some things we just can't talk about.

A: So your mother can't talk about certain things.

B: _____

A: So, you believe *you* are generally not good at communicating.

B: _____ I'm very good about communicating with most people. There are just some topics I can't bring up with my mother.

A: Because she would be angry.

B: No. _____ She's almost never angry. But she's easily hurt.

A: So, your mother makes you feel guilty for saying things that could hurt her.

B: No. _____ It's with me.

A: Ummm-hmmm.

B ▶ Role-play.

1. Work with a partner. Think of three situations—for example, between a husband and wife, a boyfriend and girlfriend, a parent and child, or a manager and an employee—in which misinterpretations might occur.
2. Write a dialogue about one of the situations. Include misinterpretations and corrections.
3. Practice your dialogue until you can perform it without reading from your paper. Add gestures and emotion and practice again. Then role-play your situation for the class.

WRITING Descriptive Writing

A ▶ Study it. Read the article and look at the photo on page 39.

> **Skill Focus: Using Descriptive Language**
> When you want a reader to enter into an experience you describe, it helps to use descriptive language—language that evokes sensory images and impressions. Appeal to the reader's imagination in terms of sight, sound, touch, taste, and smell.

1. Underline the descriptive words or phrases that enhance your sensory (sight, sound, smell, taste, touch) experience of the reading or create visual images in your mind.

2. List the words and phrases next to the appropriate sense below. Then compare your list with a partner's.

   Sight: _____

   _____

   _____

   _____

   Sound: _____

   _____

   _____

   Smell: _____

   _____

   Taste: _____

   _____

   Touch: _____

   _____

B ▶ Write it.

1. Think of an experience of a person, place, or thing that had a powerful impact on your senses. List descriptive words or phrases to describe your experience next to the appropriate sense, below.

   Sight: _____

   _____

   Sound: _____

   _____

   Smell: _____

   _____

   Taste: _____

   _____

   Touch: _____

   _____

2. Write one or two paragraphs describing your experience. Include a topic sentence for each paragraph, and make sure other sentences in each paragraph support the topic sentence. Use as much descriptive language as possible.

A Day of Discovery

It was really hot that day. You could see waves of heat. There was a light breeze, but it didn't provide much relief. It blew dust into my nose and mouth. I could smell nothing but hot sand. It was difficult to breathe. My hands and face were dry and covered with dust. My lips were cracked, and when I licked them, I tasted sand.

We were digging at the site of a tomb. Late in the day, we found the entrance. When we stepped inside, we entered a different world. The air smelled stale, but it was much cooler. Of course it was very dark. But we held up our lamps, and I felt my heart race with excitement. The walls were covered with hieroglyphics and drawings. The colors were still clear and vivid. And we could see a second opening on the far wall.

I touched the cool, rough stone at the second entrance. Then I went in. Faintly, from outside, I could still hear voices, the grinding and brushing of rock and sand, and the sounds of machinery. But inside, I was surrounded by silence. No one behind me spoke, and I was holding my breath. The light from a lantern fell on something large, and I felt excitement run through my body like electricity. In the center of the room was a sarcophagus. The drawings on it were a little faded, but that was not important. There was a body in this sarcophagus! I was just beginning to breathe again when I noticed something flash in the dark. It was gold. Ancient treasures lined the floor along the walls.

Editing Checklist

- Do your paragraphs have topic sentences?
- Do all of the other sentences in each paragraph support the topic sentence?
- How many examples of descriptive language can you find in your writing?

PUT IT TO THE TEST

A ▶ Read.

1. Read the article. Then answer the questions that follow.

The Bigfoot-Giganto Theory: Fact or Fantasy

It has many names: Sasquatch, Yeti, Kaptar, Kikomba, and Bigfoot. All over the world, there have been sightings of a mysterious creature that stands 7–8 feet tall. For hundreds of years, people have been digging for the truth about these creatures. Are they fact or fantasy?

Most researchers who accept the possibility of Bigfoot's existence favor a certain explanation of its identity: The Bigfoot-Giganto Theory. This explanation suggests that these creatures are surviving relatives of the *Gigantopithecus*. This giant ape was a cousin of the orangutan, and it stood upright eight to nine feet tall. It is believed to have become extinct more than 100,000 years ago.

So, did these creatures really survive into the 21st century? ■ Scientists admit that we do not know all the species on the planet. ■ There have been discoveries of new and supposedly extinct animals, like the coelacanth fish that were discovered in 1938 in South Africa. These fish were thought to have become extinct 70 million years ago. ■ Scientists believe that thousands of years of adaptation to temperate and mountainous climates would have given the *Gigantopithecus* the ability to tolerate cold temperatures, climb through deep snow, and cross over mountain ranges in order to survive. ■

There have been hundreds of reports of encounters with these creatures worldwide, but proving their existence is difficult. Skeptics ask why, if there are so many of these creatures around, there are not more photographs of them. Believers in Bigfoot's existence say the people involved in these surprise encounters are not in much of a position to take pictures. Either they do not have a camera at the time, or they are too frightened and confused to snap a picture before the creature walks out of view.

One thing believers and skeptics agree on is the unlikelihood that all of these reported encounters are deliberate hoaxes. There are simply too many of them, often from people unaware that anyone else has ever reported such a creature. Fact or fantasy? Time will tell.

Sources: Accessed March 2007 http://theshadowlands.net/ bf.htm# names; Accessed March 2007 from the Bigfoot Field Researchers Organization's website http://www.bfro.net/REF/THEORIES/MJM/whatrtha.asp

2. Answer these questions about the reading.

1. Look at the four squares [■] that indicate where the following sentence could be added to the passage.
   Other mythical animals, such as the Giant Panda and the Okapi (mountain gorilla), were discovered in the last century.
   Where would the sentence best fit?
   a. Choice 1
   b. Choice 2
   c. Choice 3
   d. Choice 4

2. Which of the following can be inferred from paragraph 5 about Bigfoot hoaxes?
   a. There have been many.
   b. All of the sightings have been hoaxes.
   c. None of the sightings have been hoaxes.
   d. Believers and skeptics believe in Bigfoot's existence.

3. What does the passage imply about Bigfoot's existence?
    a. There have been Bigfoot sightings all around the world.
    b. Skeptics have proven that Bigfoot is a hoax.
    c. Without hard evidence, we don't know if Bigfoot truly exists.
    d. The evidence proves the existence of Bigfoot.

B ▶ Listen.

Listen to a conversation between two friends. You may take notes as you listen. Then answer the questions.

1. Why does John tell the story about his encounter with Bigfoot?
    a. To upset his friend who doesn't believe in Bigfoot.
    b. To explain why he will not go back to the Smoky Mountains.
    c. To convince his friend that Bigfoot exists.
    d. To try to find rational explanations for his experiences.

2. What does Ted imply about rationalizing?
    a. It helps you to see the truth and overcome your fear.
    b. It is a technique used by many people.
    c. It doesn't work very well.
    d. It helps you remember.

3. According to the conversation, which of the following happened first?
    a. John told Ted about the encounter.
    b. John told other friends about the encounter.
    c. John told his wife about the encounter.
    d. John told a ranger about the encounter.

C ▶ Personal interpretation.

What are some other myths that you know about? Choose one. Is there evidence that either supports or discredits the myth? In your notebook, write a summary of the myth and your reasons for believing (or not believing) it is true. Be prepared to read your summary to the class.

D ▶ Integrated speaking.

Prepare a response to the following question. You will have 20 seconds to prepare and 60 seconds to give your response.

> In the listening section, the men discuss two possible solutions to a problem one man has. Describe the problem. Then state which of the two solutions you prefer and explain why.

Unit 4   Digging   **41**

5 Creating an Image

READING AND SPEAKING

A ▶ Warm up. Look at these company logos.
1. What brand (product or company name) does each of these logos represent?
2. What do you associate with each logo?

🎧 B ▶ Read. Scan to find the parenthetical information in the article on page 43. Check (✓) *example*, *definition*, or *extra information*.

> **Skill Focus**
> **Parenthetical Information**
> Words in parentheses usually indicate an interruption in a sentence. The purpose of the interruption can be to give examples, a definition, or extra information that isn't crucial.

	Example	Definition	Extra information
1. (who recently had a tattoo removed)	___	___	___
2. (distinctive names and trademarks)	___	___	___
3. (graphic representations of their names)	___	___	___
4. (memorable phrases)	___	___	___
5. (bags, mugs, and skins for mp3 players)	___	___	___
6. (and all the pizza he can eat)	___	___	___

C ▶ Read again. Check (✓) the reasons the people brand themselves. Base your answers on what you read, not what you infer.

	for profit	for promotion	for free stuff
1. Donna	☐	☐	☐
2. Robert	☐	☐	☐
3. Tad	☐	☐	☐

D ▶ Pair work. Discuss these questions with a partner.
1. What well-known logos can you think of? Slogans?
2. What would be a good slogan for your teacher? Your class?

Personal Branding

When Donna Ling decided to **promote** her singing career by having her logo tattooed on her arm, her father (who recently had a tattoo removed) objected strongly. "He said that branding is for corporations and cattle," Donna told us. "But I told him that, while I respected his opinions, branding today is not what it was in his generation."

We generally accept the idea of companies putting effort into creating strong brands (distinctive names and trademarks), logos (graphic representations of their names) and slogans (**memorable** phrases). Everyone recognizes brands like Mercedes, Nike, and Apple. But now people like Donna are branding themselves.

Donna chose her professional name and designed her own logo. She **came up with** *Sing-a-Ling* as her **slogan**. And is all this going to **pay off**? Well, Donna's CD sales have increased, and her performance schedule has filled up. And she started selling clothing with her **logo**. She doesn't get sales information until June, but she'll probably make as much money from the sales of clothing and other items (bags, mugs, and skins for mp3 players) as from her music this year!

Robert Falls is part of a pizza chain's branding efforts. He wears clothes with the restaurant logo whenever he is in public – and his car is covered by an ad for pizza! In return, he receives monthly payments (and all the pizza he can eat). Robert smiles and says, "My friends like to laugh at me, but I start college next year, and this is paying my tuition."

Tad Cochran is a handsome young actor. He's already on a soap opera, but his contract ends next month, and he wants to make movies. He made a deal with a famous clothing designer to wear only the company's clothes. He won't get paid, but he'll get lots of **exposure**. The company will send him to social events every month, each one attended by important people in the movie industry.

LISTENING

Match the slogans with their company or product. Then listen and check your answers.

1. _____ iPod
2. _____ Adidas
3. _____ FedEx
4. _____ Air France
5. _____ Amazon.com
6. _____ Xbox
7. _____ Nokia
8. _____ PlayStation
9. _____ DeBeers
10. _____ Jaguar

a. A diamond is forever.
b. Born to perform.
c. Connecting people.
d. Jump in.
e. Play Beyond
f. When it absolutely positively has to get there overnight.
g. Making the sky the best place on Earth.
h. 5,000 songs in your hand.
i. And you're done.
j. Forever sport.

Unit 5 Creating an Image **43**

ACTIVATING GRAMMAR

The Simple Present for the Future

Remember that *will*, *be going to*, or the present continuous can be used to talk about future time.

I start college next year, and this **is paying** for my tuition.
He won't get paid, but he'**ll** get lots of exposure.
And **is** all of this **going to** pay off?

The simple present can also sometimes be used to talk about scheduled events in the future. Verbs that can be used this way include *arrive, close, end, finish, get, go, have, leave, open, return,* and *start*. When the simple present is used for future time, often specific time words or expressions are also used.

She **doesn't get** sales information until June.
I **start** college next year.
His contract **ends** next month.

* See page 135 for additional grammar practice.

A ▶ Read. Complete the paragraph with the words in the box. You will use one word twice. Then underline the time words or expressions in each sentence.

arrives	get	meet
closes	have	

I _____ an appointment with a tattoo artist next Wednesday. I _____
       1   2
with him at 4:00 to look at designs, and then at 4:30, I _____ my tattoo. I don't know if it will
                                                          3
hurt or how long it will take, but it can't take more than a half hour because his office _____
                                                                                            4
at 5:00. After that, I _____ my friend at the airport. Her flight _____ at 7:30.
                        5   6
She'll be the first person to see my tattoo!

B ▶ Pair work. Talk with a partner about the topics below. Try to use the simple present form of the verbs in parentheses. With many other verbs, other forms for future are more natural, so it's OK to use *I'll, going to,* and the continuous in your discussion, too.

1. vacation plans (go, leave, arrive, return)
2. a doctor or dentist appointment (have, go, see)
3. a sale coming up at a place you like to shop (open, close, sale starts, sale ends)

44   Unit 5   Creating an Image

VOCABULARY

A ▶ Practice. Complete the sentences using the words in the box.

| come up with | logo | pay off | slogan |
| exposure | memorable | promote | |

1. I wonder who designed that company's _____. It's very colorful and artistic.
2. My two-year-old likes to repeat the _____ of a major toy company.
3. I like to travel to other countries just for _____ to other cultures and languages.
4. What do you think is the best way to _____ the new product?
5. I want our daughter's graduation party to be a _____ event.
6. I made some financial investments early this year. I hope they _____ later.
7. Our team is trying to _____ a way to expand into the high school market.

B ▶ Listen. Listen to five people talking. Check (✓) the things you hear them talk about.

	Brand	Exposure	Logo	Pay off	Slogan
Person 1	☐	☐	☐	☐	☐
Person 2	☐	☐	☐	☐	☐
Person 3	☐	☐	☐	☐	☐
Person 4	☐	☐	☐	☐	☐
Person 5	☐	☐	☐	☐	☐

Unit 5 Creating an Image

LISTENING The Body Mobile

A ▶ Warm up. Look at the items in the chart. Check (✓) the services you've used or received. Then discuss the experiences with a partner.

___ 1. manicure
___ 2. pedicure
___ 3. waxing
___ 4. facial
___ 5. tanning
___ 6. haircut and styling
___ 7. tattooing
___ 8. ear piercing
___ 9. other body piercing
___ 10. massage

B ▶ Listen. Cross out the services in Activity A that Leslie does NOT plan on offering as part of her new business.

Skill Focus — Fact or Opinion?
A fact is information that you can support with evidence. You can verify that it's true or that it's not. An opinion usually reflects a person's emotions or feelings about something. An opinion can also reflect a person's bias or prejudice.

C ▶ Listen again. Check (✓) whether each statement is fact or opinion.

Statement:	Fact	Opinion
1. The Body Mobile opens next month.	☐	☐
2. A mobile personal care bus is a little strange.	☐	☐
3. Now people don't have to go to different parts of town for the different services the Body Mobile will offer.	☐	☐
4. It's embarrassing to get a pedicure at the mall.	☐	☐
5. Body piercing is disgusting.	☐	☐
6. Tanning can be dangerous.	☐	☐

D ▶ **Group work.** Discuss these questions in a group.
1. Do you enjoy getting your hair cut?
2. Who cuts your nails? Do you use nail polish or get manicures? What do you think of long fingernails on women? On men?
3. Does anyone in your group have a tattoo? What does it represent for that person?
4. Do you think the image of people with tattoos is changing? If so, how?

CONVERSATION STRATEGY Asking and Answering Personal Questions

A ▶ **Pair work.** Listen and circle the answers that fit best. Then practice the conversation with a partner.

Asking

* Can I ask you a personal question?
* Would you mind if I asked you about . . . . ?
* How much do you weigh?

Answering

* Sure. Go ahead.
* It depends on what it is.
* Not at all. What would you like to know?
* Actually, I'd rather not talk about that.
* I weigh 175 pounds.
* That's a personal question.

A: Can I ask you a personal question?
B: (It depends on what it is. / Actually, I'd rather not talk about that.)
A: Why do you have the name "Julie" tattooed on your arm?
B: (Actually, I'd rather not talk about that. / Not at all. What would you like to know?)
A: No problem. But would you mind if I asked you about the tattoo on your neck?
B: (Not at all. What would you like to know about it? / It depends on what it is.)
A: Well, why did you choose a butterfly?
B: Julie loved butterflies.
A: Ah. And you loved Julie?
B: (*That's* a personal question. / Not at all. What would you like to know.)

B ▶ **Role-play.** Work with a partner. Use the sentences from Activity A to ask and answer personal questions. Use the topics below, or think of your own.
1. money
2. romance/relationships
3. health/weight
4. age

Unit 5 Creating an Image **47**

WRITING Using Graphs and Charts

> **Skill Focus: Supporting Your Writing with Charts and Graphs**
>
> Charts and graphs are sometimes used by writers as additional means of presenting information. Often a chart or graph will present data also found in the text; readers may find the visual form easier to interpret than the written words.

A ▶ Study it. Read the article and study the bar graph on page 49.

1. Underline the sentences in the article that are supported by information in the graph.

2. Double underline the percentages that are supported by the information on the vertical axis of the graph.

3. Circle the adjectives that are supported by the information on the horizontal axis of the graph.

B ▶ Write it.

1. Read the paragraph below. It contains more information from the same 2003 Harris poll. List the percentages, and write the corresponding adjectives next to them.

> People who have tattoos might be surprised to know how others see them. In 2003, fifty-seven percent of polled Americans without tattoos saw people who had them as less attractive, and forty-two percent saw people with tattoos as less sexy. Thirty-six percent of the population without tattoos thought of people with tattoos as less intelligent, and thirty-one percent saw them as less spiritual. Twenty-nine percent of the people without tattoos saw tattooed individuals as less healthy, and twenty-one percent saw them as less athletic. About eight percent of the people without tattoos felt that people with tattoos were stronger.

Percentage of People without Tattoos	Saw People with Tattoos as . . .
1. 57%	less attractive
2.	
3.	
4.	
5.	
6.	
7.	

2. Copy the paragraph in Activity 1 onto a clean piece of paper. Then make a bar graph to present the information in the paragraph. Be sure that you write the percentages on the vertical (up and down) axis, and the adjectives on the horizontal (across the bottom) axis.

Make People Feel?

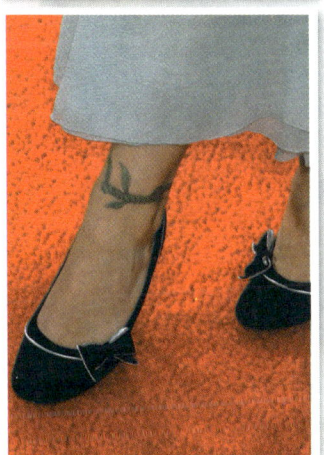

According to a Harris poll of Americans conducted in 2003, sixteen percent of the population had at least one tattoo. The poll revealed that the age group with the highest percentage of tattoos was 25- to 29-year-olds with thirty-six percent. Only seven percent of people 65 and older had tattoos.

Among the important findings in the poll, thirty-four percent of Americans with tattoos said that having a tattoo made them feel sexier. Additionally, twenty-nine percent of those with tattoos said that having a tattoo makes them feel more rebellious. Others said that having a tattoo makes them feel more attractive (twenty-six percent). But apparently tattoos won't do much for your brain or your physique. Only five percent of Americans reported that tattoos make them feel more intelligent or more athletic (three percent).

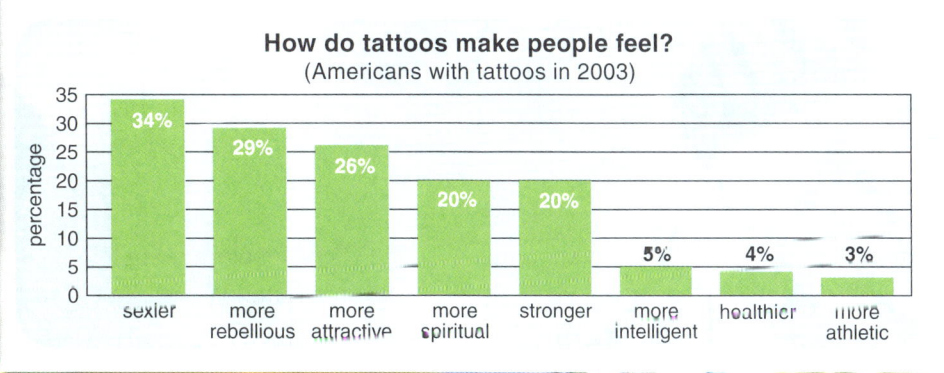

How do tattoos make people feel?
(Americans with tattoos in 2003)

Feeling	Percentage
sexier	34%
more rebellious	29%
more attractive	26%
more spiritual	20%
stronger	20%
more intelligent	5%
healthier	4%
more athletic	3%

Editing Checklist

- Is your graph clear and easy to read?
- Are the percentages on the vertical axis?
- Are adjectives on the horizontal axis?
- Does the information in the graph match the ideas in the writing?

PUT IT TO THE TEST

A ▶ Read.

1. Read the article. Then answer the questions that follow.

Body Modification

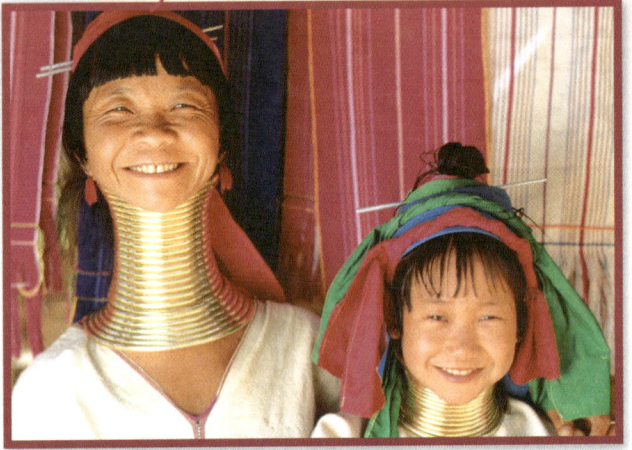

In Myanmar, the women of the Padaung Karen ethnic group wear brass neck rings to make themselves more attractive. In many up-river communities of Borneo, both men and women stretch their earlobes to indicate wealth or enhance beauty. Maori men of New Zealand get *moko* (facial tattoos) carved on their faces with a bone chisel. These customs may seem strange to outsiders, but they are not so different from the beautification practices you would find in almost any culture worldwide.

Body modification has a long history. Whether it is acceptable or not, however, depends on your culture's concepts of beauty. Elongating the neck or binding the feet might seem strange to you, but these processes have essentially the same purpose as piercing the ears for earrings. The purpose of foot-binding in China was to stunt the growth of a woman's feet so she would be more attractive to men. Some women today have foot surgery so they can fit into high-heeled shoes that supposedly make their legs look more beautiful. In either case, a woman consciously alters her body in the name of her culture's idea of beauty. Women and men may use braces to straighten their teeth, have surgery to remove body fat, or undergo operations to "fix" a nose or remove skin wrinkles. It's all in the pursuit of beauty.

Body modification can also be part of a rite of passage, such as a ceremony that marks the transition from childhood to adulthood. Or it can indicate some undesirable social status. For example, a permanent scar called a brand—made by burning the skin with a hot piece of metal— might be used to mark a person as a criminal. Some young people, especially members of college social groups called fraternities, have turned this negative symbol into a sign of something positive. As a sign of loyalty, they have been branding their arms with their fraternities' names.

2. Answer these questions about the reading.

  1. The first sentence of a summary of the passage is given below. Complete this summary by selecting the three answer choices that express the most important ideas in the passage.

  Body modification is common worldwide and has a long history.

    a. Body modification practices in other cultures seem strange because of different ideas about beauty.
    b. Foot binding was practiced in China.
    c. Sometimes, body modification is part of a rite of passage or a mark of low status.
    d. People modify their bodies mostly to enhance beauty or to express themselves.
    e. Some college students brand themselves.
    f. Some body modification is dangerous and unhealthy.

  2. The word enhance in the passage is closest in meaning to _____.
    a. discover
    b. communicate
    c. increase
    d. change

  3. The word consciously in the passage is closest in meaning to _____.
    a. intentionally
    b. involuntarily
    c. accidentally
    d. permanently

B ▶ Listen.

Listen to a lecture about beauty practices among the Padaung people. You may take notes as you listen. Then answer the questions.

1. What is the main topic of the lecture?
   a. Traditional customs as tourist attractions
   b. Reasons the Padaung people are refugees
   c. Reasons the Padaung women wear neck rings
   d. How the Padaung women have abandoned their traditions

2. How does the lecturer show the present-day usefulness of neck coils?
   a. By showing that Padaung culture is more modern
   b. By pointing out that tourists wear them
   c. By detailing the health benefits of the coils
   d. By describing the tourist value of traditional culture

3. Why does the lecturer mention the term "human zoo?"
   a. To illustrate objections to the Padaung tourist attractions
   b. To explain why the Padaung tourist attractions are illegal
   c. To demonstrate the disappearance of Padaung cultural practices
   d. To describe how the Padaung people have changed

C ▶ Personal interpretation.

Look at the picture below. What do you think of this type of body modification? Rank the following types of body modification from most shocking to least shocking. Why did you rank them in that order? Be prepared to explain your rankings to the class.

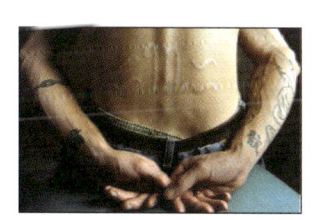

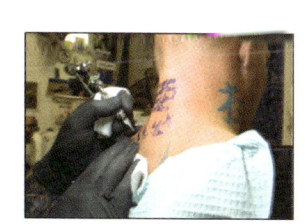

a. _____   b. _____   c. _____

d. _____   e. _____   f. _____

D ▶ Independent writing.

Write a response of about 250 words to the following prompt. Use specific reasons and examples to support your response.

   Do you agree or disagree with the following statement?

   "Beauty is not in the face; beauty is a light in the heart."

   (Khalil Gibran)

6 Things That Scare Us

READING AND SPEAKING

A ▶ Warm up.

1. Read the first two sentences of the article on page 53. What does *arachnophobia* mean? What does *phobia* mean?

2. List three phobias people might have. Complete the chart to show how the phobia might affect someone's life. For example, how might a phobia of heights affect where a person lives?

Phobia	How does it affect people's lives?
1.	
2.	
3.	

B ▶ Read. Read the article. Circle the letters of the things that happened in it.
   a. Miss Muffet sprayed her car with poison.
   b. Miss Muffet put tape on her windows.
   c. Miss Muffet hid her clothes.
   d. Dr. Hoffman asked Miss Muffet to get treatment.
   e. Dr. Hoffman used a computer as part of Miss Muffet's treatment.
   f. Miss Muffet wore a special headset and glove.

C ▶ Read again. Write the letter from Activity B next to the correct purpose or intention.

1. _____ to see and hold the virtual spiders
2. _____ in order to create a virtual world filled with spiders
3. _____ to keep spiders outside
4. _____ so that she could kill any spiders

> **Skill Focus: Identifying Words that Indicate Purpose**
>
> The words and phrases *to, in order to,* and *so that* identify the purpose or intention of an action. They enable us to answer *Why* questions about actions, for example: *Why did Miss Muffet put tape on her windows?*

D ▶ Pair work. Check (✓) the things you are afraid of. Discuss ways to cope with these fears.

____ fire
____ public speaking
____ dogs
____ flying (in a plane)

____ crime
____ shark
____ dirt
your idea: _____

Overcoming Fear

Some people like spiders, and some are nervous around them – and a few suffer from arachnophobia. Most people have little understanding of arachnophobia, but Dr. Hoffman knows a lot about it. It's one of the many phobias he helps **patients** overcome, using virtual technology.

One of his patients, nicknamed Miss Muffet, was terrified of spiders. For years, before she got in a car, she sprayed it with poison to kill any spiders. Before she went to bed, she sealed her windows with tape so that spiders couldn't come in. She kept her clothes in plastic in order to stop spiders from hiding in them. These techniques provided a little relief, but Miss Muffet was still so afraid of spiders that she became unable to leave her house. She felt lonely and sad. She was very **depressed**. Her life was becoming **unbearable**.

Miss Muffet had to do something. She finally went to Dr. Hoffman in order to get **treatment**. Dr. Hoffman used a computer to create a virtual world full of spiders. Then, he put Miss Muffet into it.

Miss Muffet wore a special headset to enter the virtual world of spiders. First, she simply watched a spider across the room. She did this every day, and **gradually** she became less afraid of it. Soon she was wearing a special glove to pick up virtual spiders.

Then, Dr. Hoffman gave her a final test. He showed her a real spider. Miss Muffet was able to hold it **confidently** in her hand! It was a **thrilling** moment for both doctor and patient.

Few people suffer from their phobias to the extent Miss Muffet did. Virtual technology has helped a few people with arachnophobia, and Dr. Hoffman is looking for ways to help people with other phobias. Perhaps phobias will soon be a thing of the past.

Hunter Hoffman holding a virtual spider near a patient.

LISTENING

Sequence the sentences numbering them 1–5. Listen to the interview and check your answers.

a. _____ David Clark's arachnophobia became unbearable.

b. _____ David Clark was able to pick up a real spider and hold it.

c. _____ David Clark decided to get treatment for his phobia.

d. _____ David Clark had a few techniques to cope with his arachnophobia.

e. _____ David Clark gradually became more comfortable with spiders.

Unit 6 Things That Scare Us 53

Activating Grammar

Quantifiers: *a few, few, a little,* and *little*

Quantifiers such as *a lot (of), most, many, some,* and *no* have obvious meanings. The quantifiers *a few, few, a little,* and *little* can be challenging.

Few and *a few* are used with count nouns.

Few people suffer from their phobias to the extent Miss Muffet did.

few = negative idea: not many at all

A few people suffer from arachnophobia.

a few = positive idea: some

Little and *a little* are used with non-count nouns.

Most people have **little** understanding of phobias.

little = negative idea: not much at all

Her techniques provided **a little** relief at first.

a little = positive idea: some

A ▶ Read. Use the quantifiers *a few, few, a little,* and *little* to complete the article.

  Speaking in public is a frightening activity for most people. In surveys, people rate public speaking as more frightening than dying! Of course, we all probably know _____ people who can speak confidently in public, but for most of us, it's unbearable.

  Unfortunately, _____ people realize there are techniques to cope with this fear.
Spend _____ time thinking about these suggestions, and gradually, you will discover that speaking in public can be thrilling! Follow these tips:

1. Keep your talk simple. In many situations, you are the expert. Of course, _____ people may have some or even a lot of knowledge about your subject, but only you have *your* viewpoint and experiences.

2. Add_____ humor. Tell a joke or funny story so that you and the audience can relax.

3. Speak more loudly than usual. People have _____ patience for quiet speakers. If they can't hear you, they'll be bored.

4. Practice in front of a mirror. _____ practice can help you notice any annoying expressions or body movement. Experienced speakers have _____ annoying habits, so try to copy an experienced speaker's arm and hand movements.

B ▶ Survey. Survey at least eight people about their fear of the things listed in the chart. Make a mark for each *yes* and each *no* answer in the chart. Present your results to the class.

Are you afraid of...	Yes	No
spiders?		
snakes?		
dogs?		
cats?		
horses?		
sharks?		

Example: *A lot of the people I interviewed are afraid of spiders, and a few of them are afraid of snakes....*

VOCABULARY

A ▶ Practice. Match the words on the left to their meanings on the right.

1. ____ virtual   a. feeling sure about your abilities or opinions
2. ____ confident   b. exciting
3. ____ depressed   c. very sad and unhappy for a long period of time
4. ____ gradually   d. a person who sees a doctor for help
5. ____ patient   e. too hard to accept or endure
6. ____ thrilling   f. happening slowly over a long period of time
7. ____ treatment   g. imaginary, or existing only electronically
8. ____ unbearable   h. medical care

B ▶ Read. Complete the paragraphs with the vocabulary words from Activity A.

Mica's Mysophobia

For years, my brother Mica had mysophobia. He was afraid of dirt and germs. To stay away from germs, he never shook hands with people or touched doorknobs. Using a shopping cart was _____ (1). Mica couldn't cope with his phobia anymore. He stopped going out, and as each month passed, he _____ (2) became quieter and more _____ (3).

Then, Mica heard about an experimental _____ (4). A doctor used a computer to create a _____ (5) supermarket full of things to touch. Mica wants to try this treatment. I am _____ (6) it will help him because he really wants to get better. He'll be a very trusting and cooperative _____ (7). It will be a _____ (8) day when he overcomes his phobia!

LISTENING Frightened by a Friend

A ▶ Warm up. Look at the photo and listen to the reporter's introduction. Circle the answers.

1. What is the story about?
   a. A snake handler was helping a friend move when a snake attacked him.
   b. A snake handler was moving a snake when it attacked him.
2. Who are Sam and Chloe?
   a. Sam is a snake and Chloe is a snake handler.
   b. Sam is a snake handler and Chloe is a snake.

B ▶ Listen. Check (✓) True or False.

	True	False
1. The handler thought he was going to die.	☐	☐
2. Safety is important at the Florida Aquarium.	☐	☐
3. It's easy to remove a biting snake from one's own body. **OR**: It's easy to free oneself from a biting snake.	☐	☐
4. The snake actually didn't have a very strong bite.	☐	☐
5. Snakes have different personalities.	☐	☐
6. Chloe was not aggressive.	☐	☐

C ▶ Listen again. Circle the example Sam gives to illustrate his point.

1. One way Florida Aquarium protects its handlers is by ____
   a. requiring all handlers to enter cages in pairs.
   b. training all handlers to recognize aggressive behavior in snakes.
2. One technique to remove a biting snake involves ____
   a. pulling the snake's mouth open and then pushing the snake away.
   b. pushing the snake's head forward and then pulling it up.
3. An example of antisocial behavior in snakes is ____
   a. hiding.
   b. attacking.
4. Sam thought Chloe was his friend because ____
   a. she came down from her tree for him.
   b. she generally liked people.

> **Skill Focus: Recognizing Supporting Examples**
> Speakers often give examples to illustrate a general statement or opinion. To recognize these examples, listen for signal words such as: *for example, for instance*, and *such as*. The listener can also ask for examples to clarify. Requests for examples include language such as: *Could you give an example . . .* and *Such as?*

56 Unit 6 Things That Scare Us

D ▶ Group work. Choose an activity. How might it become frightening? Give examples to support your ideas.

CONVERSATION STRATEGY Asking if Someone Has Time to Talk

A ▶ Pair work. Complete the conversations with phrases from the box. Listen and check your answers. Then practice the conversations with a partner.

- Is now a good time? There's something . . .
- Can I have just a little of your time . . .
- Do you have a minute? I'd like to talk to you . . .
- I'm wondering if you could spare a few minutes so that . . .
- If you have a moment, I'd . . .

Skill Focus: Asking if Someone Has Time to Talk
Sometimes a person may not be happy if you interrupt them to talk about a problem or ask for a favor without warning. It's important, and polite, to ask if someone has time to speak with you — especially if the topic is sensitive or problematic.

1. **A:** Dr. White. _____ we could talk about my assignment.
   B: I'm really busy now. Could we meet later? How about 5 o'clock?

2. **A:** Hi Jorge. _____ like to get your opinion about something.
   B: Sure. What is it?

3. **A:** Excuse me, Professor. _____ about your biology class.
   B: Yes, come in.

4. **A:** _____ we need to discuss about your job performance.
   B: Sure. What is it?

5. **A:** _____ to talk about something I'm worried about?
   B: OK. What's up?

B ▶ Role-play. Read the situations below and write a new one with your partner. Then role-play a conversation for each situation.

1. You want to ask your professor for extra time for an assignment. You are frightened to approach your professor because she is not very friendly.
2. You want to borrow money from a friend. You are uncomfortable because you have never borrowed money before.
3. (your idea): _____

Unit 6 Things That Scare Us

WRITING   Using Punctuation to Convey Tone or Emotion

A ▶ Study it. Read the paragraph about the earthquake Joe experienced on page 59. Look for punctuation that helps to express surprise, fright, important definitions or additional information, or suspense. Then answer the questions below.

> **Skill Focus**
>
> **Using Punctuation to Convey Tone**
> Good writers use punctuation to help express surprise, fright, importance, suspense, and other tones and emotions. An exclamation point (!) can indicate surprise or fright. A dash (—) alerts you to an important definition, or important additional information. Ellipses (. . .) can help to create suspense.

1. What are two surprising things that happened?
   _____

2. What are two moments of suspense?
   _____

3. What is some important factual information about the earthquake?
   _____

B ▶ Write it. Write a story about a frightening event you experienced.

1. Choose a frightening event from the list below.
   - a natural disaster
   - an encounter with an animal
   - a person who scared you
   - a financial scare
   - an accident or illness
   - (your idea): _____

2. Write notes.
   1. Something surprising about the event: _____
   2. Something suspenseful about the event: _____
   3. A definition or important piece of information that will give the reader background or a better understanding of the event: _____

3. Think about the punctuation you will use when you include the information above in your story. As you write your story, try to write sentences using exclamation points, dashes, and ellipses.

Shaken Up

I was in an earthquake once. It was years ago, but I remember it like it was yesterday. I was with my family in our car when I felt the ground begin to shake. At first, I thought something was wrong with the car—perhaps a flat tire. Then suddenly, part of the highway in front of us cracked open!

After the highway cracked, we were in shock. We waited . . . we thought we were safe . . . and then we felt another tremor! My father thought fast. We left the car and found shelter in a building near the highway. We got under tables. There was another tremor, and it lasted for several seconds . . . but it was minor. We realized we were safe, but we had to take action.

We called my aunt and uncle and arranged to meet them at a shelter. Fortunately, my parents kept an emergency kit in the trunk of the car, so we had everything we needed for a few days. We knew we were lucky to be alive. The earthquake was very powerful— it measured 6.9 on the Richter scale.

> **TIP** In a story or narrative, your paragraphs don't always need a topic sentence and supporting details. But your paragraphs should still focus on one main idea or one main event.

Editing Checklist

- Did you describe a frightening experience?
- Did you include something surprising? something suspenseful?
- Did you use an exclamation mark, a dash, and ellipses?
- Do all your paragraphs primarily focus on one idea or event?

PUT IT TO THE TEST

A ▶ Read.

1. Read the article. Then answer the questions that follow.

Cheers for Fear

Mary Johnson's fear saved her life. As she was walking to her car, a man approached her. He said that his car battery was dead and that he needed her car cables to get it started again. Just before Mary
5   opened her car door for him, she trusted her instincts. She quickly turned and ran inside a store and alerted a police officer, who later tracked the man down. The woman's instincts were right. The man had a gun, some rope, and handcuffs in his car, and his car
10 battery was working properly. From all appearances, he was planning to kidnap her.

Mary Johnson was lucky, but she was also smart. She had the good sense to act on her fear instead of squelching it, and that probably saved her from being
15 kidnapped and perhaps killed. Gavin de Becker, author of the book *The Gift of Fear* and an expert in predicting violent behavior, states that a victim of violence usually feels a sense of fear before it occurs. Some people react by distrusting this fear as irrational,
20 which is not a very sensible reaction. Others, more wisely, make use of their "gut feeling" to get out of the situation. It is important to act on your fear and to do so immediately, before you lose important survival options. Run away from a threat, search your house
25 when you hear an unusual noise, or cross to the other side of the street if you get a bad feeling about a stranger approaching you. By trusting your instincts, you can eventually learn to predict violence and therefore avoid it.

30 Fear is an instinctive reaction common to most animals. An antelope senses a lion's presence. A mouse hides in a hole from a hawk that it can't see. A person decides not to take a shortcut through a dark alley because of a bad feeling. The decisions that we make
35 on the basis of justifiable fear are hardly ill-informed and may save our lives more often than we know.

Sources: Accessed March 2007 from: http://www.amazon.com/Gift-Fear-Gavin-Becker/dp/0440226198

2. Answer these questions about the reading.
1. Five of the following items are mentioned in the reading passage as possible ways to respond to fear. Mark each as either a good (G) or bad (B) response, according to the reading. Two of the items are not mentioned in the passage as responses to fear and should not be marked.

_____ Listening to your fear instincts

_____ Considering your fear irrational

_____ Carrying a weapon

_____ Learning to predict violence

_____ Helping strangers

_____ Reacting quickly to your fears

_____ Not fleeing from a situation you fear

60   Unit 6   Things That Scare Us

2. The word he in the passage refers to
   a. the police officer
   b. the man who asked for help
   c. Mary's friend
   d. Gavin de Becker

3. The word it in the passage refers to
   a. violence
   b. fear
   c. book
   d. sense

B ▶ Listen.

Listen to a conversation between a psychologist and a patient. You may take notes as you listen. Then answer the question.

1. What is the man most afraid of?
   a. His boss
   b. Quitting his job
   c. His panic attacks
   d. Being a failure

2. Listen again to two parts of the conversation. Answer the question you hear after each part.

   1. a. As an image to show how the attacks can be useful
      b. As an illustration of the cause of his attacks
      c. As one area of work in which the man could get a job
      d. As an example of how people handle fear

   2. a. The panic attacks should scare him into opening his own business.
      b. The panic attacks are a sign that he should follow his dream and open his own business.
      c. His life is boring and he needs to change it.
      d. His life can be better if he changes his job.

C ▶ Personal interpretation.

Have you ever decided not to do something because your fear instincts told you to beware? In your notebook, write a description of the situation. What were you afraid of? Was your fear instinct correct, or was there really nothing to fear? Be prepared to read your description to the class.

D ▶ Independent speaking.

Prepare a response to the following question. You will have 15 seconds to prepare and 45 seconds to give your response. Use specific reasons and examples to support your response.

> The psychologist in the listening conversation says that fear of a major life change is an indication that the change is good. Do you agree with this advice? Why or why not?

Unit 6 Things That Scare Us **61**

7 Transformations

READING AND SPEAKING

A ▶ Warm up. Look at the photos and discuss the question.
1. What do these before-and-after pictures show?
2. How has your town or city changed in the last 20 years?

B ▶ Read. Check (✓) the statements that you can infer from the reading.

1. ___ During most of the twentieth century, people thought Bilbao was an exciting city.
2. ___ Bilbao probably has more hotels and restaurants than it did in 1993.
3. ___ Bilbao didn't have a tourist industry before the Guggenheim Museum opened.
4. ___ The Disney Concert Hall problems probably involved money and schedule.
5. ___ The Walt Disney Company was impressed by the Guggenheim, so they asked Gehry to come back.
6. ___ Gehry wasn't interested in fame or money.

C ▶ Read again.

1. Check (✓) the best paraphrase for each bold sentence.

   Throughout most of the twentieth century, there were many factories in Bilbao but there was little to attract tourists.

   ___ a. For most of the twentieth century, Bilbao had a lot of factories, but there weren't many tourist attractions.

   ___ b. Twentieth-century tourists didn't like to go to Bilbao, but there were a lot of factories.

   ___ c. Tourists didn't go to Bilbao in the twentieth century because they were not attracted by factories.

   Gehry's design made a huge impact on the selection committee, and work began eight months later.

   ___ a. Eight months after work began, the selection committee approved Gehry's design.

   ___ b. The selection committee was impressed by Gehry's design, and within eight months, work had already begun.

   ___ c. The selection committee worked eight months before Gehry's design made an impact.

2. Paraphrase this sentence:
   Basque officials wanted to change Bilbao's image and transform it into a vibrant city.
   _____

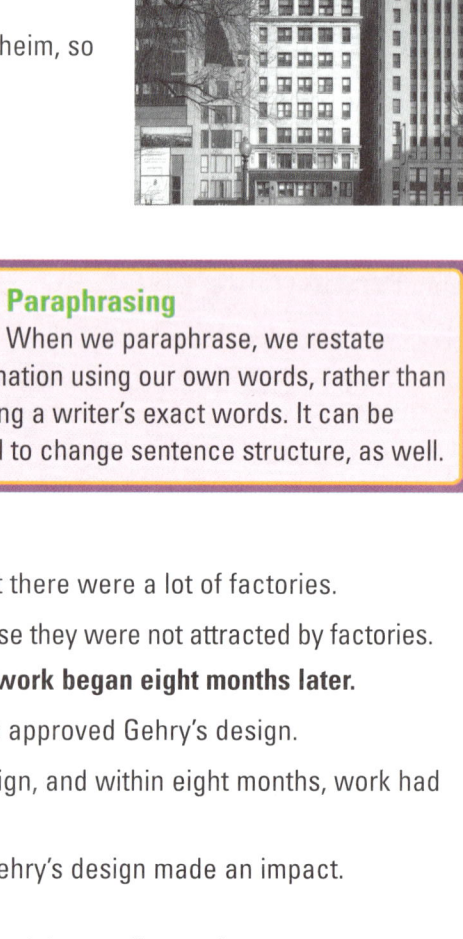

> **Skill Focus: Paraphrasing**
> When we paraphrase, we restate information using our own words, rather than copying a writer's exact words. It can be useful to change sentence structure, as well.

62 Unit 7 Transformations

Transforming Bilbao

Can one building change the life of its architect? Can one building change a city? Yes . . . if the architect is Frank Gehry, and the building is the Guggenheim Museum in Bilbao, Spain.

Bilbao is in the Basque country of northern Spain. Throughout most of the twentieth century, there were many factories in Bilbao but there was little to attract tourists. The Basque officials wanted to change Bilbao's image and **transform** it into a **vibrant** city. By 1991, the Basque leaders had decided on a plan – to get a world-class museum for Bilbao. Later that year, the Basque leaders approached the Guggenheim Foundation and proposed Bilbao as a location for a new museum. **Coincidentally**, the Guggenheim Foundation had just approved a plan to open several cultural centers. They liked the idea of building a museum in Bilbao. By 1992, the government had identified a site for the museum and a search for an architect began. Architect Frank Gehry presented his proposal in 1993. Gehry's design made a huge **impact** on the selection committee, and work began eight months later. When the Guggenheim Museum was completed, tourists flowed into Bilbao. Today the **thriving** city welcomes millions of tourists each year.

Before Gehry designed the Guggenheim, most people hadn't heard of him. Although he had been famous in the architecture world for years, most ordinary people only came to recognize his name after the Bilbao Guggenheim. He had won an important architecture prize before that, in 1989, and after winning the prize had started work on the Walt Disney Concert Hall in Los Angeles. But in a short time, the project **encountered** many difficulties and many people **blamed** Gehry. The Bilbao Guggenheim offered Gehry an escape from the problems of the Disney project and he succeeded **triumphantly**. This work was finished within its budget and on schedule. Gehry then completed the Disney concert hall. Interestingly, when it was finished, many people said Gehry had copied his Guggenheim style!

D ▶ Pair work. Discuss the following with a partner.
1. The transformation of another city or place
2. Something that might change your town or city in positive ways

LISTENING

Listen to a resident of Bilbao talk about the city. Then check (✓) what he thinks is positive and negative.

	Positive	Negative
1. The opening ceremonies of the Guggenheim Museum	☐	☐
2. Driving in the city	☐	☐
3. Enjoying a cup of coffee in a café	☐	☐
4. The price of housing	☐	☐
5. The new airport	☐	☐
6. How people feel about the city	☐	☐
7. The new jobs and businesses	☐	☐
8. General life in the city	☐	☐

Unit 7 Transformations

ACTIVATING GRAMMAR

The Past Perfect and the Simple Past

We use both the simple past and the past perfect to talk about the past. We use the past perfect (*had* + past participle) to show that something happened before another event or before a specific time in the past.

By 1992, the Basque government **had identified** a site for the museum, and a search for an architect **began**.   First they identified the site. Then they began the search for an architect.

Before Gehry **designed** the Guggenheim, most people **hadn't heard** of him.
   First people didn't know about Gehry. Then he designed the Guggenheim.

*See page 135 for additional grammar practice.

TIP — Signal Words and Dates
Look for signal words or dates to determine the order of events. *By the time, when, before* and *after* all show changing times.

A ▶ Read. Complete the paragraph with the simple past or past perfect form of the verb in parentheses.

A New Friend

By the time Harold Krause _____ (die) in 2007, he and his wife Anna
                                1
_____ (be) together for 50 years. Harold's death _____ (have)
       2   3
a big impact on Anna. Throughout her life, Anna _____ (be) a vibrant and
                                                         4
active woman, but after Harold's death she _____ (find) herself unable to get
                                                    5
out of bed. Her family worried. Anna _____ (not / be) any better although ten
                                              6
months _____ (pass). Anna began seeing a doctor. The doctor
            7
_____ (see) many patients like Anna before. At one point, he
       8
_____ (recommend) that Anna take a vacation, but Anna refused. As
       9
she was driving home from his office one day, a small dog _____ (run)
                                                                    10
suddenly into the street. Anna's daughter pulled the car over. Fortunately the car
_____ (not / hit) the dog. The dog was dirty
       11
and alone. Anna decided to keep it. She named it Trixie and
_____ (walk) it every day. In a short
       12
time, Anna looked much better. Actually, she
_____ (not / feel) so good in a
       13
long time. Thanks to their coincidental encounter, both Anna and Trixie are thriving.

64 Unit 7   Transformations

B ▶ Listen. Listen to the sentences. Then check (✓) which event happened first.

1. a. ___ Anna made her decision.
   b. ___ Anna went for her last doctor's visit.
2. a. ___ Anna found Trixie.
   b. ___ Anna gave up hope of feeling better.
3. a. ___ Two weeks passed.
   b. ___ Anna felt better.
4. a. ___ Anna had Trixie for two weeks.
   b. ___ Anna began to feel better.
5. a. ___ Anna didn't like dogs.
   b. ___ Anna found Trixie.

VOCABULARY

A ▶ Practice. Match the words on the left to their meanings on the right.

1. ___ blame
2. ___ coincidentally
3. ___ encounter
4. ___ impact
5. ___ vibrant
6. ___ thriving
7. ___ transform
8. ___ triumphantly

a. successfully, showing confidence
b. doing well
c. meet, find
d. impression, influence
e. by accident
f. say someone is responsible for something bad
g. alive, exciting
h. change

B ▶ Discuss. Discuss the following topics with a partner. Use the vocabulary from Activity A.

1. Transformations in your life or other transformations you have seen or heard about
2. Something that had a big impact on you
3. A vibrant or thriving area or business in your city
4. A time when you were blamed for something unfairly
5. A coincidental encounter with someone that led to something good

LISTENING Cat Woman

A ▶ Discuss. Look at the photo. What is your impression of this woman? What look or image is she trying to present? What do you think this listening is about?

Jocelyn Wildenstein

🎧 B ▶ Listen. Answer the following questions.

1. How much money has Jocelyn spent on plastic surgery?

2. Where on her body has Jocelyn had plastic surgery?

3. Where was Alec's home in Africa?

4. What were two of the wild cats Alec had on his land?

5. How many children did Jocelyn and Alec have?

🎧 C ▶ Listen again. Then number the sentences in the correct sequence.

a. ____ Jocelyn and Alec got married and had children.
b. ____ Jocelyn had plastic surgery.
c. ____ Jocelyn went to Kenya, Africa, with Alec and owned and hunted wild cats.
d. ____ Alec divorced Jocelyn.
e. ____ Alec started to lose interest in Jocelyn.

> **Skill Focus: Sequencing**
> When we sequence events, we put them in order of what happened first, second, third, and so on. Look for words and phrases like *first, in the beginning, before, after that, in the end,* and *now* to help you identify the sequence.

66 Unit 7 Transformations

D ▶ Group work. Discuss these questions with your classmates.

1. What are reasons that people have plastic surgery?
2. Would you consider having plastic surgery? Why or why not?
3. What do you think about Jocelyn's decision to have plastic surgery?

CONVERSATION STRATEGY Getting to the Point

🎧 **A ▶ Pair work.** Complete the conversations with sentences from the box. Listen and check your answers. Then practice the conversations with a partner.

> * **So, it sounds like** you don't like the changes she's made.
> * **I guess the important thing is that** she's happy with him.
> * **So what you're getting at is that** working at home is convenient.
> * **So your point is that** you want to break up with me?
> * **The thing I want to say is that** I've tried everything.

Skill Focus: Getting to the Point
Sometimes when a conversation has gone on for a while, we want to find out what the main point is. It is important to do this politely.

1. **A:** Have you seen Tami? She dyed her hair and she's acting like a teenager. She wears clothes I wouldn't let my daughter wear.
   B: _____

2. **A:** I can't quit smoking. I tried chewing gum. I tried wearing a patch. I tried going cold turkey—you know, just stopping suddenly.
   B: So what are you going to try next?
   A: _____

3. **A:** Sam told me you're thinking of quitting your job to work at home. I'll tell you, I'm so glad I did this! I have more time to take care of myself — to cook and exercise. I don't have to wear nice clothes. I don't have to drive or take the train.
   B: _____

4. **A:** My 77-year-old mother wants to get married! I think maybe the man wants her money.
   B: Maybe she loves him.
   A: I don't know how she can forget my father like this.
   B: Maybe this new man makes her feel young again. Or maybe he helps her focus on the future. Maybe living in the past makes her sad. Maybe she needs companionship.
   _____

5. **A:** I can't go on like this. You make plans with me, but then you break them. When I'm with you at your apartment, you only want to watch TV. You never buy me anything, and you never talk to me. You're not nice to me in front of your family.
   B: _____

B ▶ Role-play. Work with a partner. Student A, talk about a change you've seen someone make or a change you've made yourself. Keep talking until your partner interrupts you. Student B, try to get to the point of the conversation. Use the expressions from Activity A. Then switch roles.

Unit 7 Transformations **67**

WRITING Shifting Verb Tenses

A ▶ Study it. Study the personal essay on page 69.

1. Discuss these questions with your classmates:
   - What was the big, important change in the writer's life?
   - How was the writer's life different before and after the change?

2. Underline the verbs describing things that happened after the writer moved to the city.

3. Double-underline the verbs describing things that happened before that point in time.

B ▶ Write it.

1. Describe a big or important change you made in the past.
   a. Identify the change. Choose one of these ideas, or choose one of your own.
      - went to college
      - moved from one town or city to another
      - got married
      - moved from my family's house to an apartment
   b. List the way some things were before the change, and how they were different after the change.

   Before

   _____
   _____
   _____
   _____
   _____

   After

   _____
   _____
   _____
   _____
   _____

2. Write your personal essay. Pay attention to using verbs in the simple past or the past perfect.

Skill Focus

Shifts in Verb Tense

A writer will often shift verb tense to help the reader understand changes in time frames. But too many shifts in tense, or inaccurate or inconsistent shifts, can cause confusion. Good writers choose one main verb tense and indicate changes in time frame by shifting tense *relative* to the main tense.

Example: I moved to this city in 2005, and after that I made a lot of changes in my life. I hadn't taken the train or bus to work until I came here. Now I never drive.

The main verb tense is the simple past. The writer primarily describes events that happened after he moved to the city. The point of change, the move, is something completed in the past. *Moved, made,* and *came* all describe actions completed in the past.

But the writer also contrasts things that happened after he came to the city with things he did before he moved and things he does now. To help readers understand the shifts in time, the writer shifts the verb tense.

The past perfect describes events that took place before a specific time in the past. In this case, the specific time in the past is the time when the writer moved, so when he describes things that happened before that time, he uses the past perfect (*hadn't taken the train*).

The simple present is used to describe the writer's experience now. (*Now I never drive.*)

A Change of Place

Sometimes one big change brings many smaller changes. I moved to this city in 2005, and after that I made a lot of changes in my life.

I hadn't taken the train or bus to work until I came here. Before, I had driven my car everywhere. But after I moved to the city, I sold my car. Parking was expensive, and it took a long time to drive from place to place! So I started taking the subway, the bus, or taxis.

I'd spent most of my free time at the homes of my relatives or friends when I lived in my hometown. But I didn't know anyone when I moved here, so I went out almost every night. I went to restaurants, to cheap movies and plays, and to parks. I made some friends, and we started going to clubs together. I enjoy my social life now. I don't like to stay home.

At first I had problems with the noise in the city. I could hear neighbors, traffic, or music constantly. I couldn't sleep at night because of noises on the street. But I got used to the sounds of the city, and now I don't notice them. Now, I'm nervous when things are too quiet.

I'm glad I moved here. I have friends now, and I enjoy having so many things to do. Sometimes I miss my old life in the country. But I could never go back.

Editing Checklist

- Did you identify one big change?
- Did you describe things that were different after the change?
- Did you use the correct verb forms to show shifts in time?

PUT IT TO THE TEST

A ▶ Read.

1. Read the article. Then answer the questions that follow.

Pets Changing Lives

John Meyers was diagnosed with epilepsy, a chronic neurological condition, when he was 8 years old. People with epilepsy often have seizures, during which they lose some control of their bodies. John did not have many seizures when he was young, but after he turned 20, the number increased. After collapsing in a grocery store one day, John was afraid of being by himself. He felt imprisoned by his epileptic seizures. Then he met Buddy and his life changed.

Buddy is a seizure-alert dog. This type of dog is trained to activate an electronic alert system when someone has a seizure, and to stay near the person until help arrives. There have been accounts that some dogs can smell or sense a seizure before it even begins, but this theory is still being researched. Specially trained assistance dogs provide independence for people who have physical and mental disabilities. The ability to do things without the aid of another person can change people's lives. These dogs serve as the hands, ears, or eyes of their human partners. They help them perform everyday tasks that would be difficult or impossible to do on their own.

Dogs are not the only animals that can transform someone's life. Cats, horses, monkeys, and even birds are known to help people with both physical and mental disabilities. Capuchin monkeys are small, quick, and clever, and they can help people who are paralyzed. These monkeys perform essential tasks for living alone, such as turning on and off the lights, picking up dropped objects, and even simple cooking.

Animals can also be great therapists. In animal-assisted therapy programs, a companion animal may visit with hospital or nursing home patients or be a live-in pet for elderly people. Pet therapy has been proven to help people with depression, Alzheimer's disease, and other mental conditions. Because they depend on the sick or disabled person for food and affection, pets often give such a person a sense of purpose and fulfillment. Animals can also minimize feelings of loneliness and isolation and change people's outlook on life.

Sources: Accessed April 2007 at http://advocacy.britannica.com/blog/advocacy/2007/01/service-animals-help-humans-live-fuller-lives; Accessed April 2007 at http://www.epilepsy-cf.org/seizure_dogs.htm

2. Answer these questions about the reading.

1. Which of the following best expresses the essential information in the highlighted sentence? Incorrect answer choices change the meaning in important ways or leave out essential information.
   a. Pets rarely change a person's attitude about life.
   b. Taking care of assistance dogs is a lot of work.
   c. Pets make people happy.
   d. People feel they have a reason to live when they own a pet.

2. Which of the following can be inferred about John's life after meeting Buddy?
   a. John and Buddy are good friends.
   b. Buddy has improved John's life.
   c. Buddy is difficult to take care of.
   d. John is still nervous about going out alone.
3. Which of the following can be inferred about seizure-alert dogs?
   a. Researchers are still not sure whether they can sense a seizure coming on.
   b. It is proven that they can sense a seizure before it happens.
   c. Only a few dogs can sense a seizure coming on.
   d. They can prevent seizures by alerting a patient.

B ▶ Listen.

Listen to a lecture about helpful animals. Then answer the questions.

1. What is the main topic of the lecture?
   a. Horse therapy
   b. Dolphin therapy
   c. Myths about pet therapy
   d. The benefits of pet therapy

2. Listen again to two passages from the lecture. Then answer the question after each passage.
   1. a. He believes it usually works.
      b. He hasn't seen any evidence that it works.
      c. He believes it worked for his friend's son.
      d. He believes it can be dangerous for some patients.
   2. a. Supporters of pet therapy believe some animals naturally know how to help people.
      b. Supporters of pet therapy believe animals can sense things people cannot sense.
      c. Animals use real data to evaluate the needs of humans.
      d. Humans can learn how to communicate their needs to animals.

C ▶ Personal interpretation.

Can animals sense the way humans are feeling? What makes you think they can or cannot? Do you think animals have the ability to help heal humans? Prepare a two-minute spoken response to these questions.

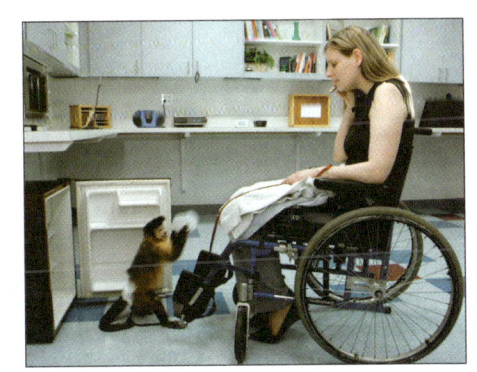

D ▶ Integrated writing.

Summarize the points made in the lecture, being sure to specifically explain how they strengthen points made in the reading passage. Your response should be about 175 words. You have 20 minutes to plan and write your response.

Unit 7 Transformations 71

8 Frozen

READING AND SPEAKING

A ▶ Warm up. Skim the article on page 73 and look at the photos. Predict what the article will tell you about McMurdo Station.

B ▶ Read. Read the article.
1. Check your prediction(s) from Activity A. Were they correct?
2. Check (✓) the true sentences about McMurdo Station and the people working there.

___ Most of the people living at McMurdo are not researchers.

___ There are about 150,000 people at McMurdo.

___ Elaine Frye does not enjoy living at McMurdo.

___ Elaine is a photographer, and she loves taking pictures in Antarctica.

C ▶ Read again. Look at the chart. Which column is the better basis for a summary? Check (✓) the column.

Skill Focus: Summarizing

When you summarize, you use your own words to restate what an entire reading, or an entire section of a reading, is about. It's important to change some of the vocabulary and sentence structures. A summary should focus only on the main idea and a few important details. A summary should not include your opinions. Summarizing will help you understand and remember what you read.

___ A	___ B
McMurdo is like a tiny city. It's cold, but it's a very wonderful place to live.	McMurdo—research station in Antarctica. Some scientist, but most people are support staff (drives, cooks, . . .)
Some people just want to experience Antarctica and then go home.	Has services and entertainment (airport, hospital, restaurants, golf, . . .)
Sometimes 1,000 people live in McMurdo.	Number of residents grows from around 200 (winter) to 1,000 (summer)
It's wonderful to see the animals in Antarctica, especially for photographers.	Some people take time off from jobs in the United States to come to McMurdo.
I think I would like to live in McMurdo for a while, but I would get bored like Tommy.	Some enjoy the experience, but some are glad it's temporary.
New people are waiting for the opportunity to replace the ones who retire.	A lot of people are waiting for the chance to live in McMurdo.

Life in Antarctica

McMurdo is a U.S. research station in Antarctica. When you think of people at a research station, you probably think of scientists. But most workers at McMurdo are support **staff**—drivers, cooks, construction workers, computer technicians, and many others all help to keep the station in operation. With an airport, a hospital, restaurants, bars, a library, a movie theater, and a golf course, McMurdo is like a **tiny** city.

The population ranges from about 200 people in the winter to nearly 1,000 in the summer. Some people who come to McMurdo during the summer months have successful careers in the United States, but they take time away from them to come to McMurdo. Their jobs at McMurdo may be less **demanding** and interesting than their jobs back home, but they provide a chance to experience life in Antarctica.

Elaine Frye took a year off from her teaching job to come to the station. "I could have stayed home and had a nice life. Who knows, I might have had a great year at my school. Here, I wash dishes in a restaurant. That may sound boring, but I'm **having a blast**." In her time off, Elaine takes photos of the penguins, small birds, and other animals. Elaine says. "Yesterday I took a picture of two killer whales! I really think this could be the greatest place in the whole world. I'll miss it when I go home. I might try to come back again in a few years."

Tommy Long has been at McMurdo almost six months, and he looks forward to returning to his **permanent** job. "I like it here, but it's getting a little boring, and I want to leave before I get **sick of** it. It's a great experience, but I've been here long enough. I'm sure somebody else will **be dying to** take my place."

Tommy is probably right. There is a long list of people waiting for the **opportunity** to live in one of the coldest places on Earth.

D ▶ Pair work. Work with a partner. Use the information from the correct column in Activity C to practice giving summaries. But use your own words, and try to use complete sentences.

LISTENING

Listen to two summaries of the reading. Check (✓) the better summary.

___ Summary A   ___ Summary B

ACTIVATING GRAMMAR

Modals of Possibility

We use *could/couldn't*, *may/may not*, and *might/might not* to talk about possibility in the present.

> This **could** be the coolest place to live in the whole world.
> Elaine **couldn't** be at work yet. It's not even 8 A.M.
> Washing dishes in Antarctica **may** sound boring, but I love it.
> It **might not** be warm enough outside to go for a hike right now.

We use *could*, *may/may not* and *might/might not* to talk about possibility in the future.

> I **could** get sick of this place after a year.
> Elaine **might** even try to come back again in a few years.
> They **may not** like living in Antarctica, so maybe they shouldn't come.

When we talk about something that was possible in the past, we use *could have*, *may have*, or *might have*.

> I **could have** stayed there and had a nice life.
> Elaine **might have** found a boyfriend if she had stayed in San Francisco.

* See page 135 for additional grammar practice.

A ▶ Read. Read the blog about Happy Camper School. Circle the correct modals.

February 11
Happy Camper School

Yesterday was our first day at Happy Camper School. It (might be / may have been) the hardest day of my life. All the new staff members at McMurdo Station have to come here to learn how to survive on the ice. People usually spend
5 two nights here, but we (might stay / might have stayed) an extra day because we started late yesterday.

First, we had to learn how to stay warm. It's an important lesson to always keep in mind, because a person in freezing weather like this (could get / could have gotten) very ill.
10 Next, we put up tents. Then, we had to build an ice "house" made out of snow. I didn't sleep in it last night because there wasn't room, but I (may sleep / might have slept) there tonight. It (could get / could have gotten) a little scary, though, because I don't like small spaces!

B ▶ Speaking. Complete the sentences with your own ideas. Then explain them to your partner.

1. It's _____ o'clock now, so the _____ could be closed.
2. Next weekend, I might _____.
3. _____ may be the most important decision I make this year.
4. I could have _____ last weekend, but I didn't.
5. Our teacher might have _____ when he/she was a student.

74 Unit 8 Frozen

VOCABULARY

A ▶ Practice. Circle the best meaning of the bold words.

1. Working in a café is a **demanding** job because you deal with customers all day.
   a. very easy
   b. very hard
   c. really enjoyable

2. He **was dying to** tell her about the party, but he couldn't because it was a surprise.
   a. was very eager to
   b. was too sad to
   c. didn't want to

3. I didn't expect to have a good time, but actually I'm **having a blast**.
   a. having a bad time
   b. feeling bored
   c. having a lot of fun

4. She accepted the job because it was an **opportunity** to work with interesting people.
   a. chance
   b. choice
   c. job

5. I'm **sick of** my job. I need to find a new one.
   a. tired of
   b. absent from
   c. worried about

6. Our company has a big **staff**. We have about 800 employees.
   a. team of players
   b. group of cleaners
   c. group of workers

7. Dan's not living with us **permanently**. He'll move when he finds an apartment.
   a. responsibly
   b. forever
   c. for a short time

8. The diamonds in these earrings are so **tiny** that you can't see them.
   a. dark
   b. very small
   c. cheap

B ▶ Listen. Listen to the woman talk about being a professional ice sculptor. Complete each sentence with a word from Activity A.

1. Sylvia is _____ making ice sculptures for weddings and parties.
2. Someday, she hopes to have a _____ to help her.
3. She thinks the car sculpture was a good _____ to show off her work.
4. The most demanding job she ever did was to make 100 _____ birds for a fancy party at the zoo.
5. Sylvia is _____ the cold.

A car made entirely of ice

Unit 8 Frozen

LISTENING Through the Snow

A ▶ Warm up. Listen to the beginning of the conversation. Then answer the questions.
1. Why does Rita want to slow down?
2. Who is driving?
3. Where are they going?

B ▶ Listen. Circle the answer to each question.
1. Why is Jay driving fast?
   a. they're early b. they're late c. they're lost
2. Why can't they see the exit sign?
   a. it's raining hard b. it's snowing c. it's dark outside
3. Where are they going?
   a. to Maplewood Ski Resort b. to Rita's house c. to a concert
4. Who was supposed to pack the directions?
   a. Rita b. Jay's brother c. Jay
5. Why can't Rita use her cell phone?
   a. Jay forgot to pack it b. Rita forgot to pack it c. it's not working

> **Skill Focus: Using Context Clues to Infer a Speaker's Feelings**
> We can often use context clues to make inferences about how a speaker feels. A confident speaker may express certainty and talk positively about his or her abilities, using language such as "Yes, of course I can." and "I am a great artist." An unsure speaker might say something like "uh . . . , um . . . ." and "I don't know." A depressed speaker might use phrases such as, "I wish we had . . ." or "And all because . . ."

C ▶ Listen again. Read each question and check (✓) the correct feeling. For each question, tell which sentence in the box gives context clues to help you decide.

> a. Or, um . . . it might be a different one.
> b. You'll be great.
> c. And all because I didn't bring directions.
> d. I'm great at it.

1. How does Jay feel about his driving?
   ___ confident ___ depressed ___ unsure
   Which sentence helps you decide? _____

2. How does Rita feel about using Exit 28?
   ___ confident ___ depressed ___ unsure
   Which sentence helps you decide? _____

3. How does Jay feel about the possibility of missing his brother's wedding?
   ___ confident ___ depressed ___ unsure
   Which sentence helps you decide? _____

4. How does Rita feel about the speech Jay is going to give?
   ___ confident ___ depressed ___ unsure
   Which sentence helps you decide? _____

D ▶ **Pair work.** Discuss the following with a partner.
- a time you felt confident
- something you are unsure about
- something that frustrates you, such as an activity, a school subject, or a person

CONVERSATION STRATEGY Expressing Tentative Agreement

A ▶ **Practice.** Complete the conversation with phrases from the box. Listen and check your answers. Then practice the conversations with a partner.

> * **That might be a good idea,** as long as you don't think she'll be mad.
> * **I think so,** but I'd like to find out more about it.
> * **That could work,** but why don't we talk in the morning?
> * **That's probably the best way to approach it,** but let me think about it.

1. **A:** I don't think I can go skiing with you tomorrow. I have to go to the library and do some research.
   B: Why don't you go in the morning? We could go skiing in the afternoon.
   A: _____.

2. **A:** It might snow tonight. Do you think we should cancel dinner with my mom?
   B: _____
   _____. Last time we canceled, she was furious.

3. **A:** I'm so sick of my boss. He never thanks his staff and he always yells at us. I might write him an email telling him how I feel. What do you think?
   B: _____.

4. **A:** So, do you agree with Mom? Do you think I should take the job in Antarctica?
   B: _____. It sounds like a good opportunity, but I don't know much about the lifestyle there.

B ▶ **Pair work.** Work with a partner. Practice the target expressions by completing the conversations.
1. **A:** I might tell the professor that my other classes are too demanding, and I'd like an extra week to write my paper. What do you think?
   B: That's probably the best way to approach it, but . . .
2. **A:** I may reduce my hours at work so I have more time to study.
   B: That might be a good idea . . .
3. **A:** Will you be able to help me with _____ tomorrow?
   B: I think so, but . . .

WRITING Writing More Effective Summaries

A ▶ Study it. Read the first paragraph of the article "Deep Freeze" on page 79. Then read the summary.

1. Underline the topic sentence in the article. Underline the topic sentence in the summary.

2. Underline other information in the article that is included in the summary.

3. Is the information in the summary presented in the same order as the information in the article?

___ yes   ___ no

> **TIP Writing a Summary**
> Writing a summary is similar to giving a spoken summary. State the main idea and key information in your own words. Present information in the same order as in the material you're summarizing. Be brief. Include only facts—not your inferences or opinions.

B ▶ Write it. Write a summary of the paragraph "How did he die?"

1. Underline the topic sentence, the three supporting sentences, and the concluding sentence in the paragraph.

2. Write the topic sentence and the three supporting sentences in the left column of the chart below. In the right column, restate these sentences in your own words.

Original Sentences	Restated in Your Own Words
Topic sentence:	
Supporting sentence 1:	
Supporting sentence 2:	
Supporting sentence 3:	
Concluding sentence:	

3. Use the information in the chart to write a summary of the article.

Summary

On the border of Italy and Austria, in 1991, the frozen body of a 5,300-year-old man was found. The media named him Ötzi. Scientists discovered that Ötzi had been 46 years old and 5'3" (165 cm) when he died. Ice froze his body and the items he carried with him, such as clothes, tools, and food. By studying Ötzi, scientists have learned many things about people who lived in 3,300 B.C.

Deep Freeze

Who is Ötzi?

In 1991, the frozen body of a 5,300-year-old man was discovered in the mountains on the Italy-Austria border. The news media quickly gave the body a name. They called him Ötzi, after the area where two German tourists found his body. Scientists examined Ötzi's body and answered many questions about his identity. They learned that Ötzi had been 46 years old and 5'3" (165 cm) tall when he died in approximately 3,300 B.C. The scientists guessed that ice covered Ötzi's body shortly after he died. The ice completely froze his body. Fortunately, the ice also preserved Ötzi's possessions, which included: a coat made of woven grass, leather shoes and a leather vest, a knife, an axe, and berries. Because of Ötzi, scientists have learned a great deal about how people lived 5,300 years ago. But there are still many questions.

How did he die?

Until recently, there were three major theories about Ötzi's death. One theory was that Ötzi was killed as part of a religious ceremony, or sacrifice. A second theory was that Ötzi might have died in a snowstorm. There is evidence in the Earth's geographical history that there was a great storm around the time of his death. A third explanation for his death was that Ötzi died in a fight. This explanation has been supported by recent research. A bit of an arrow was found in his body. The location of the arrow matched a small tear in Ötzi's coat. In addition, bruises and cuts were found on Ötzi's hands, wrists, and chest. Although there are still questions about specific details concerning his death, there is strong evidence to suggest that a fight was the cause.

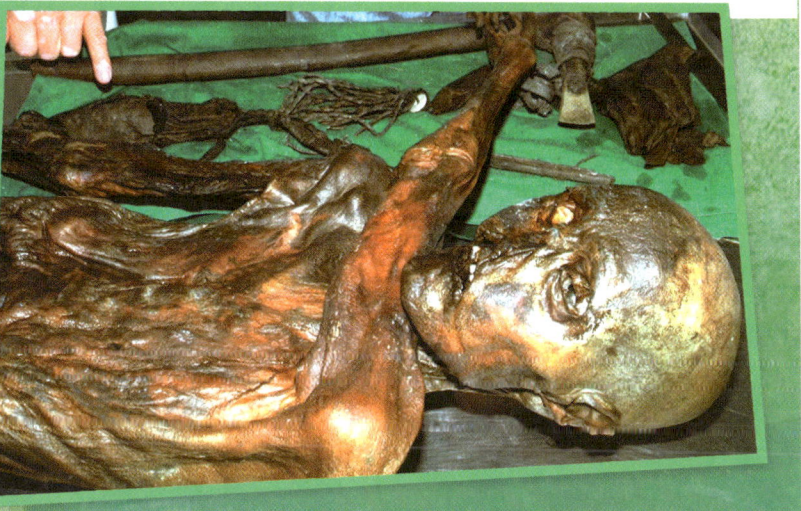

Editing Checklist

- Compare your own topic sentence to the topic sentence in the original paragraph. Does it include the same information?
- Is the information in your summary presented in the same order as the information in the article?
- Did you state only the facts, and none of your personal opinions?

PUT IT TO THE TEST

A ▶ Read.

1. Read the article. Then answer the questions that follow.

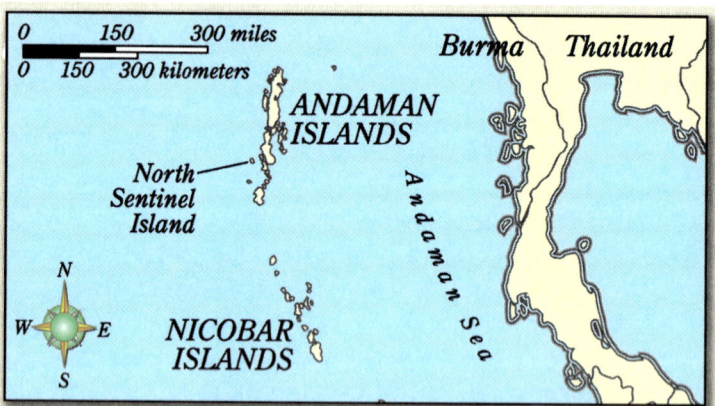

Privacy Please

On August 2, 1981, the *Primrose*, a ship carrying poultry feed, got stuck beside a tiny island in the Andaman Sea near Burma. The sailors saw some men come out of the forest threatening them with spears, bows and arrows. The frightened sailors took cover on their damaged ship. Until they were rescued a week later, they kept makeshift weapons like pipes and flare guns at their sides in case of an attack. This may sound like a tale from 1781 instead of a news story from 1981, but time seems to be frozen on North Sentinel Island and for its inhabitants, the Sentinelese.

Nobody has had long-term contact with the Sentinelese. They are one of the most isolated and unassimilated peoples on Earth. It appears that their social practices have had little influence from the outside world. The Sentinelese maintain their independence and isolation by refusing personal contact with outsiders and attacking any outsider who comes near their island.

Their total population is estimated at between 50 and 200 people. As hunters and gatherers, the Sentinelese hunt wild pigs, catch fish with arrows and collect wild plants and coconuts. They wear no clothes except for belts made out of leaves and vines. Since they have to rely on natural materials to make tools and weapons, metal work is rare. It has been observed, however, that they have made use of metal materials that wash up on their shores. It is their isolation from the world that has preserved their culture. According to Survival International, a group that supports isolated people, if the Sentinelese open up to outsiders, their unique identity and culture will disappear. Experts believe there is a pattern after first contact is made between a "lost" tribe and the rest of the world. Forced relocation, loss of culture and language, disease, alcoholism, and depression are all possibilities when an isolated group meets the rest of humanity.

Sources: Robin McKie, "Survival comes first for the last Stone Age tribe world," *The Observer*, February 12, 2006. Accessed March 2007 at http://observer.guardian.co.uk/world/story/ 0,,1708016,00.html; Adam Goodheart, "The Last Island of the Savages" 2000, accessed March 2007 at http://www.andaman.org/BOOK/ reprints/goodheart/rep-goodheart.htm http://www.survival-international.org/ related_material.php?id=92

2. Answer these questions about the reading.

1. Where do the Sentinelese people live?
   a. Myanmar
   b. on a ship
   c. on a beach
   d. North Sentinel Island

2. According to the passage, Sentinelese _____.
   a. refuse contact with outsiders
   b. want to be friends with outsiders
   c. depend on outsiders for food
   d. get sick from outsiders

3. The word tiny in the passage is closest in meaning to _____.
   a. undiscovered
   b. very small
   c. big
   d. dangerous

80 Unit 8 Frozen

B ▶ Listen.

Listen to a conversation between two friends. You make take notes as you listen. Then answer the questions.

1. Why does Sandy know so much about the Amish people?
    a. She learned about the Amish while she was in school.
    b. She visited the Amish country a few years ago.
    c. She is an Amish person.
    d. She heard about the Amish people on TV.

2. What does Sandy imply when she said her trip to the Amish country was very inspiring?
    a. She learned a lot about their history.
    b. She learned how to live by candlelight.
    c. She had a great tour guide.
    d. She thought the simple life of the Amish people was wonderful.

3. What does George imply when he said that he doesn't want to be an "ugly tourist?"
    a. He doesn't want to be rude and insensitive to the Amish culture.
    b. He wants to dress in plain clothes.
    c. He wants to drive a horse and buggy while he is visiting the Amish country.
    d. He wants to dress nicely while he is visiting the Amish country.

C ▶ Personal interpretation.

Do you think isolated societies like the Sentinelese and the Amish are better off without much contact with outsiders? Should outsiders continue to try to contact them? In your notebook, write one or two paragraphs answering these questions. Be prepared to read your piece to the class.

D ▶ Integrated speaking.

Prepare a response to the following question. You will have 20 seconds to prepare and 60 seconds to give your response.

> In the listening section, two people discuss possible solutions to the man's problem. Describe the problem. Then state which of the two solutions you prefer and explain why.

9 Brains

READING AND SPEAKING

A ▶ Warm up.

1. Check (✓) the things that you know about the brain. Then tell a partner.

   _____ the parts of the human brain

   _____ the size of a human brain compared to other animals' brains

   _____ what the human brain can do

2. Look at the picture in the article on page 83. What do you think the object in the brain is?

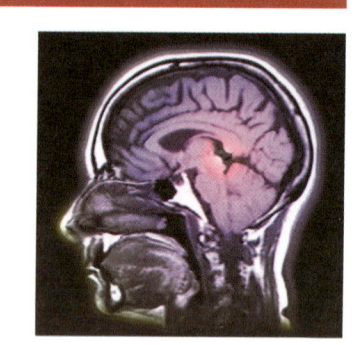

B ▶ Read. Read the article. In the chart below, check Fact, Opinion, or Not in the reading.

	Fact	Opinion	Not in the reading
1. For now, scientists are using the chip just to replace the hippocampus.	☐	☐	☐
2. Bernard Frankel wants scientists to study the brains of other animals.	☐	☐	☐
3. Putting these chips in people's brains could be very dangerous.	☐	☐	☐
4. Padma Larkin wrote a new book about the dangers of technology and medicine.	☐	☐	☐
5. Computer chips in brains will only help people.	☐	☐	☐

C ▶ Read again.

1. Check (✓) the best description of the writer's point of view.

   _____ a. an objective point of view

   _____ b. a positive point of view

   _____ c. a negative point of view

2. Underline the words and phrases in the article that indicate the writer's point of view.

> **Skill Focus: Identifying a Writer's Point of View**
>
> A point of view is the position from which someone looks at something. The topic of this article is computer chips that can be put inside the human brain. Scientists mentioned in the article have a positive point of view, perhaps because of their belief in the benefits of science. Padma Larkin is the author of a book about the dangers of technology and medicine. Perhaps because of previously formed beliefs, she has a negative attitude toward the chips. The writer of this article reveals his own point of view when he uses words like *dangerous*, *valuable*, and *intelligent* – words that show his judgments or feelings.

82 Unit 9 Brains

Wiring the Brain

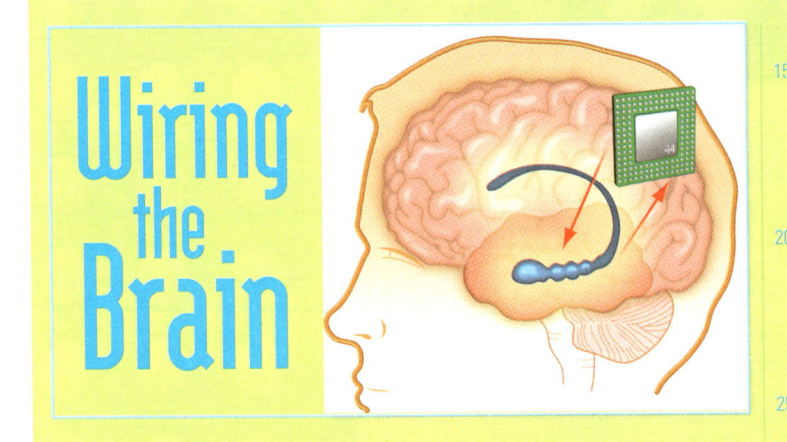

Researchers at the University of Southern California are developing a computer chip for the brain. The small plastic chip will help people whose brains are damaged, for example, victims of brain disease or serious accidents. The chip will take over the
5 work of the damaged part of the brain.

For now, researchers are focusing on using the chip for the functions of just one part of the brain: the hippocampus. This is the part of the brain that helps us create long-term memories. It "codes" new experiences and then sends them to other parts of the
10 brain to be stored. For people who are **incapable** of remembering things for very long, this computerized hippocampus could be very important.

At first, this chip sounds wonderful. But it raises serious questions. The brilliant medical journalist Bernard
15 Frankel asks, "What if brain chips make people remember terrible things that they really want to forget? It's **unclear** what would happen." It's quite possible the chip could have more negative effects than positive ones.

Another issue is making sure the chips are used
20 responsibly. Our brains control our personalities, so putting computer chips in them could be extremely dangerous. For example, what if a government or a medical company programmed the chip to make people think a certain way? There's too much potential for
25 **unethical** use of the chip.

"It's a scary concept," says Padma Larkin, an expert on personal identity whose valuable new book talks about the dangers of technology and medicine. "We know that some people program computers to do awful things," says
30 Larkin. "Look at all the viruses that destroy computers. It's **impossible** to know where this technology will lead."

Some scientists who support the brain chip dismiss these concerns. They say the criticism is **unfair**, and that the chip will only help people. But intelligent people like
35 Padma Larkin think it is **unacceptable** to give doctors the power of controlling our brains. There are too many questions that need to be answered. Perhaps these questions will be answered soon. But if they are, it will be by a person—not by a computer chip.

D ▶ Pair work. Discuss the questions with a partner.
1. What do you think about the chips the article discusses?
2. Is there anything in your background or experience that might cause you to have a certain point of view?

LISTENING

Listen to the sentences. Check (✓) the person from the reading who is discussed in each sentence.

The author	Researchers	Bernard Frankel	Padma Larkin
1.			
2.			
3.			
4.			
5.			

ACTIVATING GRAMMAR

Restrictive Adjective Clauses

We can combine two sentences using a restrictive adjective clause. This clause gives information that we need to identify the noun. We use *that, who, which,* and *whose*. We do not use commas.

> Some scientists dismiss these concerns. They support the brain chip.
> Some scientists **who support the brain chip** dismiss these concerns.
>> We need the clause to identify these specific scientists.
>
> Look at all the viruses. These viruses destroy computers.
> Look at all the viruses **that destroy computers.**
>> We need the clause to identify these specific viruses, as opposed to other viruses.

* See page 135 for additional grammar practice.

A ▶ Read. Read the article below. Then combine each sentence pair in green type into one sentence using a restrictive adjective clause. Write the new sentences.

A Full Life with Half a Brain

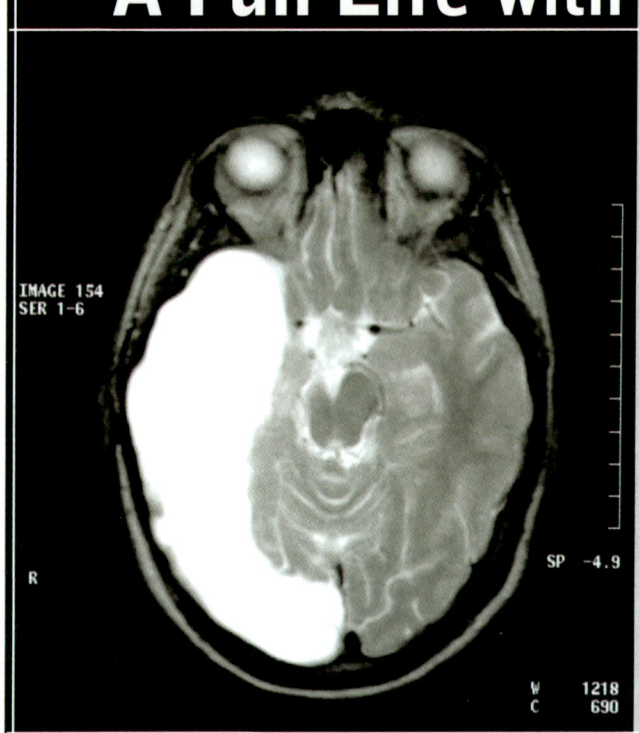

For the past twelve years, Christina Santhouse has had only half a brain.

As a young girl, Christina got a virus in her brain. (1) She had terrible seizures. The seizures made her entire body shake uncontrollably. Her doctors said they needed to remove the infected part of her brain. So when Christina was eight years old, doctors removed the entire right half, or hemisphere, of her brain. (2) Shockingly, Christina is now a college student. She can do almost everything her classmates do.

Christina isn't the only one. (3) There are other young people. Their brains were partially removed. Jeremy Sizemore was twenty when doctors took out his left hemisphere. Today, three years later, he's doing fine. (4) "A lot of people hear about my surgery. They are surprised that a person with half a brain can speak, write, and learn." Sometimes people stare at him. They say, (5) "That's the guy! He has only half a brain."

1. She had terrible seizures that made her entire body shake uncontrollably.
2. _____
3. _____
4. _____
5. _____

84 Unit 9 Brains

B ▶ Pair work. Look at the pictures. Talk with a partner about the types of people who are right for each job.

Question: What kind of people make good brain surgeons?
Answers: People who aren't afraid of blood.
People who are. . . .
People who can. . . .
People who like. . . .

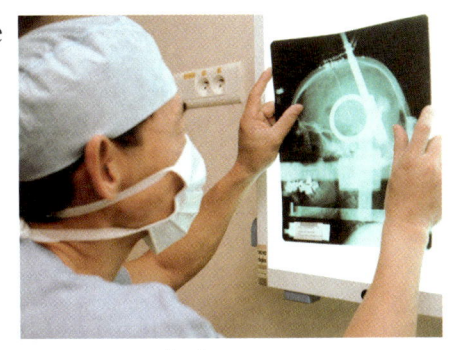

brain surgeon

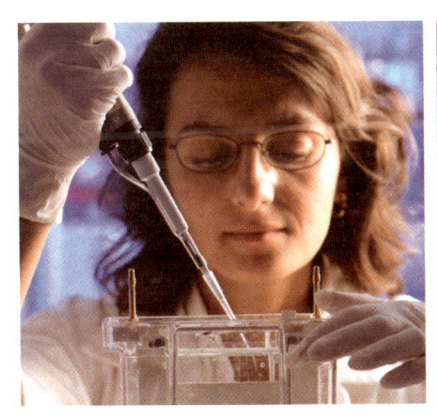

brain researcher

biology professor

science journalist

VOCABULARY

A ▶ Practice. Circle the correct words.

1. Human brains are (capable / incapable) of incredible things.
2. The facts he presented in his essay were (correct / incorrect), so he had to go back and correct them. He really wanted his essay to be (perfect / imperfect).
3. She's so (consistent / inconsistent)! One day she does great work, the next day she doesn't!
4. Most (successful / unsuccessful) businesspeople think laziness is (acceptable / unacceptable), so they only hire people who are motivated.
5. It's (possible / impossible) to get into that club unless you're famous. I think it's really (fair / unfair).
6. He was fired for (ethical / unethical) behavior after his boss discovered he was stealing money from the company. It was (clear / unclear) how long ago it had begun.

> **TIP** **Prefixes: *im-*, *in-*, and *un-***
> Prefixes help us get an idea about a word's meaning. When you see the prefixes *im-*, *in-*, and *un-* before an adjective that has its own meaning, they often mean *not or without*. For example: *unsuccessful* means *not successful*. These prefixes usually carry a negative meaning

🎧 **B ▶ Listen.** Listen to Adam King tell his roommate about his unsuccessful attempts to become a brain surgeon. Check (✓) True or False for each sentence.

	True	False
1. Adam is worried that becoming a brain surgeon is impossible.	☐	☐
2. The information Adam had about Javix College was incorrect.	☐	☐
3. Adam thinks that taking chemistry classes is the perfect solution to his problem.	☐	☐
4. Adam feels that the college has been fair.	☐	☐
5. Adam's roommate thinks the dean is incapable of giving good advice.	☐	☐
6. Adam feels that online courses are always high in quality.	☐	☐

Unit 9   Brains

LISTENING The Mozart Effect

A ▶ Warm up. Look at the pictures. Then discuss the questions in a group.

1. Why do you think the woman is playing music for her baby?
   a. to calm her baby
   b. to make her baby smarter
   c. to make her baby grow

2. What do you think the Mozart Effect is?
   a. a way for babies to learn how to write music
   b. a way for people to appreciate music
   c. a way for people to get smarter by listening to music

B ▶ Listen. Listen to Professor Harris talk about the Mozart Effect. Check (✓) the facts that you hear about each study.

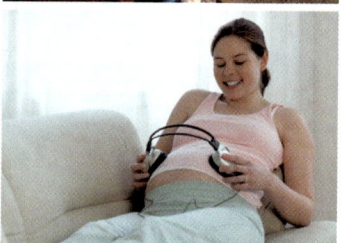

Study	Facts
1. 1993 study	a. ____ Two American scientists did the study. b. ____ The scientists learned to play Mozart's music. c. ____ Their study said that people who listen to classical music become smarter. d. ____ Their study said that listening to classical music for 10 minutes makes the brain better at solving math problems. e. ____ This theory is known as the Mozart Effect.
2. 1999 study	a. ____ This was done by the same researchers who did the 1993 study. b. ____ This was done by a new group of researchers. c. ____ They tried to repeat the study and were successful. d. ____ These researchers said the 1993 study was wrong.
3. 2004 study	a. ____ This was done by the same researchers who did the 1993 study. b. ____ This study showed that Mozart's music affects the brain. c. ____ This study showed that people who are relaxed learned more easily.

C ▶ Listen again. Check (✓) the best conclusion you can draw from Professor Harris's lecture.

____ a. People who listen to classical music are smarter than people who don't.

____ b. Listening to music increases brain power for 15 minutes.

____ c. Listening to music can have some effect on the brain, but it is still unclear how much.

____ d. The researchers who did the 2004 study were more intelligent than the ones who did the earlier studies.

Skill Focus: Drawing a Conclusion

When we draw a conclusion, we make a logical final inference about information we read or hear. While we listen, we make inferences about the main idea, the information or facts supporting the main idea, and the point of view of the speaker. At the end, we evaluate our collection of inferences and draw a logical conclusion from them.

D ▶ Vocabulary. Complete the sentences about the listening. Use words with the prefixes *in-* or *un-* from Vocabulary Activity A on page 85.

1. Many people who heard about the study didn't understand it. They _____ thought that listening to classical music would make them more intelligent!
2. The results of the 1999 study were _____ with the results of the 1993 study.
3. The new researchers who tried to repeat the original study in 1999 were _____.

CONVERSATION STRATEGY Making Excuses

A ▶ Pair work. Complete the conversations with expressions from the box. Listen and check your answers. Then practice the conversations with a partner.

> * I got stuck in traffic.
> * I'd love to, but I have to. . . .
> * I had an emergency. . . .
> * I completely forgot. . . .

1. **A:** They're giving free intelligence tests in the student lounge. Do you want to come?
   B: _____ help my roommate. He broke his leg last week and it's hard for him to get around without me.

2. **A:** Daniel, I've been waiting for you all morning. I thought you were going to bring me your research about how brain size affects intelligence.
   B: I'm so sorry, Professor Grimaldi. _____ to bring it today. But I promise I'll remember it tomorrow.

3. **A:** Hi! Sorry I'm so late. _____.
   There was a flood in my apartment!
   B: Oh no. Is everything all right?
   A: Yeah, now it is. But I forgot how crazy it is during rush hour.
   On the way here, _____.

B ▶ Role-play. Role-play the situations. Speaker B should use phrases and expressions from Activity A. Be sure to switch roles.

1. **A:** (You are a student inviting Speaker B to a movie.)
   B: (You can't go.)
2. **A:** (You are the president of a company that pays a lot of money.)
   B: (You are a college graduate who really wants to work at the company, but you were late for the interview.)
3. **A:** (You are a neighbor who wants to be friends with Speaker B. You invite Speaker B to a dinner party.)
   B: (You don't like Speaker A, but you want to be polite.)

WRITING Adding Information to Expand on an Idea

A ▶ Study it. Read the paragraph on page 89.

1. According to the author, what are six ways to boost your brain power?
   1. _____
   2. _____
   3. _____
   4. _____
   5. _____
   6. _____

> **TIP** **Introducing Additional Information**
> Use these words and phrases to add information: *additionally; also; is also a (good way to) . . .; another (thing / way, etc.); a second / third / fourth (technique / thing / way, etc.); a final (thing / way, etc.); for example; in addition to.*

2. Read the Tip box. Then circle the words or phrases in the article that introduce additional information.

B ▶ Write it. Write a how-to paragraph that gives four to six options or suggestions for doing something.

1. Choose a topic from the list, or think of your own topic.
   - How to Study for a Test
   - How to Improve Your Memory
   - How to Make New Friends
   - How to Live a Healthy Life
   - How to Organize Your Time
   - Your idea: _____

2. Write the four to six options or suggestions, along with reasons or explanations.

What to Do	Why
1.	
2.	
3.	
4.	
5.	
6.	

3. Write your how-to paragraph. Complete this sentence to use as your topic sentence:

   There are _____ things you can to do to _____.

Unit 9 Brains

How to Boost Your Brain Power

There are six things you can do to make your brain more effective. One thing you can do is sleep a full eight hours. According to scientists, people who don't sleep enough at night make more mistakes at work than people who get at least eight hours of sleep. In addition to sleeping eight hours, it is important to eat a breakfast that includes protein, such as eggs or meat. This gives the brain the energy it needs to work hard. A third way to boost brain power is exercising for at least fifteen minutes each day. Scientists from the University of Illinois found that walking every day boosted brain power by 15 percent. Keeping focused is also a good way to make the brain more effective. Dr. Glenn Wilson from London University says that people who do two or three tasks at the same time are usually unsuccessful at all the tasks. For this reason, don't try to write emails while you are on the phone and eating lunch. Another technique for increasing brain power is using your brain to solve puzzles or try new things. Throughout the day, try to spend at least 10 minutes solving crossword puzzles, playing online brain games, or making small changes to your daily habits. For example, simply brushing your teeth with your other hand can be enough to make a difference in your brain power. The final thing you can do is to be more loving. Dr. Richard Davidson says that feeling love and kindness for other people helps the brain become more efficient. Following all six of these steps every day could boost your brain's performance. It's not impossible to make your brain stronger!

Editing Checklist

- Does your topic sentence indicate the number of options or suggestions you give for doing something?
- Does your paragraph include four to six options or suggestions?
- Did you use a variety of words and phrases to add information?

Unit 9 Brains

PUT IT TO THE TEST

A ▶ Read.

1. Read the article. Then answer the questions that follow.

Brain Fingerprinting

Terry Harrington was convicted of murder in 1978 and was serving a life sentence in prison. Throughout his imprisonment, he said he was innocent. In 2003, he was released from prison and is now a free man. He can thank
5   his memory and a new technology called brain fingerprinting for his freedom.

Clues to innocence or guilt are found in the brain. Perpetrators (people who commit a crime) have details of the crime stored in their memory. Brain Fingerprinting
10 Laboratories, Inc. has developed technology that determines whether or not specific information is stored in a person's memory. The test measures brain wave responses to pictures or words associated with the crime scene. When the human brain recognizes certain information, it
15 triggers a specific electrical signal called a MERMER. This signal can be measured and analyzed to prove whether the suspect has the crime in his memory. Since an innocent person did not commit the crime, no memory of it will be found in the brain. The murder that Terry
20 Harrington was wrongly convicted for took place in a field with high grass and tall weeds. The results of Terry's brain fingerprinting test showed that the record stored in his brain did not match the crime scene but it did match his alibi of being at a concert the night of the murder.

25 Polygraphs (lie detectors) measure physical and emotional reactions to questions. Increases in pulse, blood pressure, breathing rate, and sweat levels are believed to be signs of guilt. Critics of polygraphs say that some people can trick the lie detector while nervous people could be
30 seen as guilty. During a brain fingerprinting test, pictures or words from the crime scene come up on a computer screen. If this same information is stored in the person's memory, the brain will recognize it, whether the person wants to or not. The brain wave will be the sign of memory.

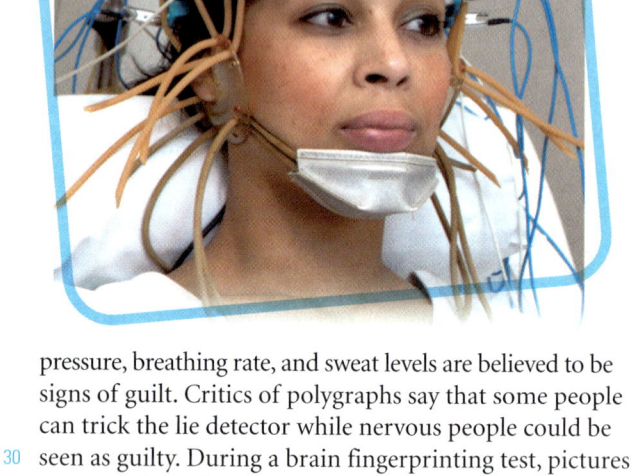

Sources: Accessed March 2007 at http://www.brainwavescience.com/ExecutiveSummary.php; Accessed March 2007 at http://www.brainwavescience.com/NewYorkTimes.php; Accessed March 2007 at http://www.brainwavescience.com/CBS%2060%20Min%20High.php

2. Answer these questions about the reading.

1. The author discusses Terry Harrington's murder case in order to _____.
   a. show that brain fingerprinting has helped free innocent people
   b. demonstrate the reliability of brain fingerprinting
   c. show that brain fingerprinting doesn't work
   d. support Terry Harrington

2. Why does the author mention polygraphs?
   a. To show that brain fingerprinting is comparable to polygraphs
   b. To explain that polygraphs are more reliable than brain fingerprinting
   c. To show that polygraphs are not as effective as brain fingerprinting
   d. To introduce another tool that is just as effective as brain fingerprinting

3. The word it in line 19 refers to _____.
   a. the signal
   b. the crime
   c. the brain
   d. the memory

90   Unit 9   Brains

B ▶ Listen.

Listen to a lecture about brain functions. You may take notes as you listen. Then answer the questions.

1. Executive skills in general are _____.
    a. business management abilities
    b. the frontal lobes of the brain
    c. brain functions used in performing tasks
    d. the good and bad traits of one's personality

2. What does the lecturer imply about doing tasks that require your weaker executive skills?
    a. Your chances for success will decrease.
    b. Your skills will become stronger.
    c. Your personality can hide these weaknesses.
    d. Your stronger skills will become weaker.

3. According to the lecturer, what is the relationship between personality traits and executive skills?
    a. Personality traits may contribute to executive skills.
    b. Executive skills may contribute to personality traits.
    c. They achieve the same results, but in different ways.
    d. One is valuable in everyday life and the other at work.

C ▶ Personal interpretation.

Imagine you have spent three years in prison for a crime you didn't commit. Then you are freed after brain fingerprinting shows your innocence. What would you do after being released from prison? How do you think your unjust imprisonment would affect the rest of your life? Prepare a two-minute spoken response to these questions.

D ▶ Independent writing.

Write a response of about 300 words to the following prompt. Use specific reasons and examples to support your response.

Do you agree or disagree with the following statement?

The chief function of the body is to carry the brain around.

—Thomas A. Edison

Unit 9   Brains   **91**

10 Keeping Secrets

READING AND SPEAKING

A ▶ Warm up. Look at only the illustrations for the story on page 93. Discuss the questions.
1. What type of story do you think it is?
2. What do you think happens in the story?
3. What do you think is the relationship between the characters?

B ▶ Read. Scan the story to answer these questions.
1. What was stolen?
2. What is believed to be at risk as a result of this theft?
3. Why did Devlin request Agent XTC for the detective job? Which of your ideas from Activity A were correct?

C ▶ Read again. Read the page from the graphic novel and the inferences in the chart. Check (✓) the correct column.

Skill Focus: Making Inferences Based on Visual and Written Information
When we read, we can make inferences based on both the text and visual images (such as illustrations, graphs, or photos). It is important to consider both sources of information. Good readers integrate the information they get from both sources.

Inference	Based on text	Based on illustration	Based on both
1. The police don't know about the theft.	☐	☐	☐
2. Devlin thinks XTC is a man.	☐	☐	☐
3. Agent XTC knows Devlin.	☐	☐	☐
4. XTC'c colleagues know the identity of XTC.	☐	☐	☐

D ▶ Group work. Create an ending to the story. Include answers to the following questions.
1. What does XTC mean by "This is only the beginning"?
2. Why does Devlin want to learn the identities of the agents?
3. What happens to Devlin and XTC's relationship?

Chapter 7: Is Agent XTC safe at last?

XTC, you've been chosen for an important, **confidential** mission. Ace System's President, Jack Devlin, has reported that a list of security codes was stolen from his office last night. Ace Systems provides these codes to companies and government agencies. Devlin wants the thief caught, and he wants us to **handle** it. He doesn't want the police involved. He requested you for the job. Many government computers, including ours, are **at risk** until we know what codes he has. Our own security is **compromised**.

I understand. I'm on my way.

Inside Jack Devlin's office at Ace Systems....

Agent XTC here. The situation's not good. The place has been **turned upside down**.

So this is XTC! We finally meet! I've waited a long time to **get rid of** him!

Careful, Agent XTC. Our camera has **detected** movement. You may not be alone.

I know. I'm being followed.

Devlin! You **disgust** me.

Good work, XTC. It all makes sense now. It was a trap. The office was set up to look like it had been robbed. The call was fake. Devlin was after **you**! Some mistakes were made on our end. We believed him too quickly. But Devlin has been caught, and you're no longer **at risk**.

I'm not so sure.... This is just beginning.

LISTENING

Listen to the end of the story and put the sentences in order from 1 to 4.

_____ a. Devlin catches Agent KZQ.

_____ b. Agent XTC tries to rescue KZQ.

_____ c. Agent XTC quits her job.

_____ d. Devlin discovers XTC is his daughter.

ACTIVATING GRAMMAR

The Passive Verb Form

Passive voice sentences focus on the **action**, not on the person or thing doing the action. We form the passive with the verb *be* and the past participle. We usually choose the passive voice when the performer of the action is unknown or unimportant. We also choose the passive voice when we want to avoid mentioning who did the action. In some cases, the passive is used when the performer of the action is clear or obvious.

I **am being followed.**	I don't know who is following me.
Some mistakes **were made** on our end.	We don't want to say who made them.
The room **has been turned upside down.**	Clearly the thief or thieves did it.

* See page 135 for additional grammar practice.

A ▶ Read. Choose the correct verb form. Then look at the sentences with the passive forms. Why was the passive used in those sentences?

When Pierre Boom was 17 years old, he found out that he wasn't a typical West German teenager. He was the son of spies for the East German government.

Early one morning, the police (raided / were raided)₁ Pierre's house. His parents and grandmother (took / were taken)₂ away and Pierre (left / was left)₃ alone with several government agents. The agents (searched / were searched)₄ the house from top to bottom. Pictures (removed / were removed)₅ from the walls. Pieces of soap (took / were taken)₆ from the bathroom, and even Pierre's bedroom (turned / was turned)₇ upside down. Later that day, Pierre (saw / was seen)₈ his father on TV. His father (had identified / had been identified)₉ as a spy. Both of his parents (put / were put)₁₀ on trial and his father (found / was found)₁₁ guilty of spying. The entire West German government (had compromised / had been compromised)₁₂ because Pierre's father had confidential information. Pierre's father couldn't handle his son's questions about the spying, and their relationship was never the same. Pierre (remembers / is remembered)₁₃ the father from his childhood. He (doesn't know / isn't known)₁₄ the man who was arrested.

Unit 10 Keeping Secrets

SPEAKING

Proverbs are famous quotations or sayings that give advice or express an obvious truth. Discuss the meanings of these proverbs in groups.

- Man's affairs are evaluated only after his coffin is closed. (South Korea)
- As you see yourself, I once saw myself; as you see me now, you will be seen. (Mexico)
- The only things that can be taken out of the bag are things that are in it. (Brazil)
- He who cannot agree with his enemies is controlled by them. (China)

VOCABULARY

A ▶ Practice. Circle the best meaning for each bold word.

1. Please don't share my idea with anyone. It's **confidential**.
   a. certain b. expensive c. secret
2. The best person for the job is someone who can **handle** difficult situations.
   a. deal with b. stop c. move
3. Soo-Jin's job is **at risk**. Her company has been sold, and her job is being cut.
   a. likely to stop b. in danger c. under attack
4. Someone discovered Leo's password, so now the security of his email account has been **compromised**.
   a. put in danger b. agreed c. taken away
5. Kevin **turned** the room **upside down**, but he still couldn't find the key to the safe.
   a. left a mess searching for something b. rearranged things in a confusing way c. removed things without asking
6. The thief tried to **get rid of** his footprints, so the police wouldn't follow them.
   a. hide b. remove c. repair
7. Mr. Oh can **detect** dishonesty in anyone's behavior. You should tell him the truth.
   a. identify b. look for c. become angry about
8. I can't be friends with people who lie. Lying **disgusts** me.
   a. attracts b. makes one sad c. makes one feel sick or upset

B ▶ Listen. Read the items then listen to the responses. The responses are not in order. Write the letter of the correct response next to the correct number.

1. _____ When I found out he'd lied to me, I was disgusted. I didn't want his presents.
2. _____ Oh that's not good. We could be at risk of losing now.
3. _____ Definitely! The thieves turned the room upside down, but they didn't find it.
4. _____ Actually, yes. I'm not pleased with the way things are being handled.
5. _____ Why not? Doesn't the company trust employees with confidential information?

Unit 10 Keeping Secrets **95**

LISTENING   What's at risk?

A ▶ Warm up. In groups, brainstorm a list of jobs that you believe people can fake. Brainstorm a second list of jobs you believe people can't fake.

🎧 B ▶ Listen. Listen to the conversation about Rick's résumé and job search. Check (✓) True, False, or Not in the listening.

	True	False	Not in the listening
1. The new résumé can lead to more job opportunities that are more exciting.	☐	☐	☐
2. Rick thinks he may not succeed at designing logos.	☐	☐	☐
3. Rick believes everyone lies on their résumé.	☐	☐	☐
4. Being caught in a lie and embarrassing his family worries Rick.	☐	☐	☐
5. The new résumé could lead to a better paying job.	☐	☐	☐
6. Rick doesn't feel guilty about having to lie in the interview.	☐	☐	☐

🎧 C ▶ Listen again. Write the numbers of the most important advantage and disadvantage Rick considers.

> **Skill Focus: Evaluating Advantages (pros) and Disadvantages (cons)**
>
> There are advantages (pros) and disadvantages (cons) for most situations. People often make decisions by weighing the pros and cons. They often specify which of the pros or cons is the most important factor in deciding. Comparative and superlative language is common in these situations.

1. Most important advantage (pro) of using the new résumé: _____
2. Most important disadvantage (con) of using the new résumé: _____

Unit 10   Keeping Secrets

D ▶ Group work. Talk with two or three classmates. When, if ever, is it acceptable to keep a big secret from your family or close friends? Describe a time when you or someone you know did this.

CONVERSATION STRATEGY Ending a Conversation

A ▶ Pair work. Complete the conversations with the expressions and sentences from the box. Listen and check your answers. Then practice with a partner.

* Oh, speaking of time, . . .
* Is it that time already? I'd better get going.
* That's a wonderful story. I'd like to hear more, but. . . .
* I know this is really upsetting for you, but can we talk later?

Skill Focus: Ending a Conversation
Sometimes we need or want to end a conversation. It is more polite to signal that we are ending the conversation than to end it suddenly. The signal can show an interest in the conversation, and may include reasons for ending it or an offer to continue it later.

1. **A:** It's almost 11:00.
   B: _____

2. **A:** I know he'll be sorry he broke up with me. He'll get tired of his new girlfriend.
   B: _____
   _____
   _____
   I need to get home.

3. **A:** . . . so my great-great grandfather moved to Texas, where he married my great-great grandmother.
   B: _____
   _____
   _____
   I have to get going.

4. **A:** You're lucky. I'm always working or taking care of my family. It must be nice to have time for a hobby.
   B: _____ I only have 10 minutes to catch my train.

B ▶ Role-play. Read the situations below and write a new one with your partner. Then role-play a conversation for each situation.

1. You run into a colleague while you are shopping. You want to talk about someone in the office who you don't like. Your colleague is not comfortable talking with you about this person.
2. You're outside telling a neighbor about a terrific vacation you took recently. Your neighbor needs to end the conversation to cook dinner.
3. You're talking about _____, but the other person _____.

Unit 10 Keeping Secrets **97**

WRITING Writing a Character Description

A ▶ Study it. Read the character description on page 99.

1. Which paragraph describes Agent XTC's personality? Which describes her physical characteristics? Label the paragraphs.

2. Check the physical and personality characteristics the writer describes.

Physical characteristics

___ age   ___ height   ___ weight   ___ hair
___ eyes   ___ ears   ___ nose   ___ mouth
___ skin   ___ strength ___ voice   ___ clothing
___ other?: _____

Personality characteristics

___ likes   ___ dislikes   ___ weaknesses   ___ strengths   ___ opinions   ___ other?: _____

> **Skill Focus**
> **Writing a Character Description**
> Character descriptions are important in short stories and other forms of creative writing. They include information about the character's physical characteristics and personality so that readers can *see* and *know* the character. Details and specific examples help the character to come alive in the mind of the reader.

B ▶ Write it. Look at the illustrations of the other two characters on the next page. Write a character description of one of them or another character of your choice.

1. Complete the chart with information about the character you chose.

Physical characteristics
1.
2.
3.
4.
5.
6.
Personality characteristics
1.
2.
3.
4.
5.
6.

2. Write the character description. Organize it in two paragraphs.

98 Unit 10 Keeping Secrets

Who is Agent XTC?

Agent KZQ Jack Devlin Agent XTC

    At only twenty-five years old, Agent XTC doesn't look like a secret agent. She has an open expression, and her bright smile and green eyes are wide. She has a small nose and smooth skin. Her thick red hair is long and straight, but it's often pulled back or up. She prefers a simple hairstyle. Agent XTC's clothes are also simple. She prefers loose and comfortable clothes made of cotton, and when she's working, she is always dressed in black.
5 Agent XTC is just five feet three inches tall and weighs 110 pounds. She appears weak and delicate, but this isn't the case. She works out every day, and she can handle any difficult situation. She can also be dangerous. She was trained in karate and she is permitted to kill, if necessary.

10 When Agent XTC isn't working, she is an ordinary twenty-five-year-old woman who likes to have fun with her friends. On weekends, she and her friends usually go to the trendiest nightclubs. Agent XTC loves loud music and Latin dancing, and she is good at salsa and samba. She and her friends also go shopping a lot. This can be a problem for her because she can't get rid of anything! Her closets are filled with coats, handbags, and shoes. Sometimes she has to turn her place upside down just to find a shoe. She is a little disorganized in her
15 personal life! However, her friends love her because she is very generous and she'll do anything for them.

Editing Checklist

- Have you clearly organized the characteristics in two paragraphs?
- Have you given enough information to enable the reader to *see* the character?
- Have you given enough information to enable the reader to *know* the character?

PUT IT TO THE TEST

A ▶ Read.

1. Read the article. Then answer the questions that follow.

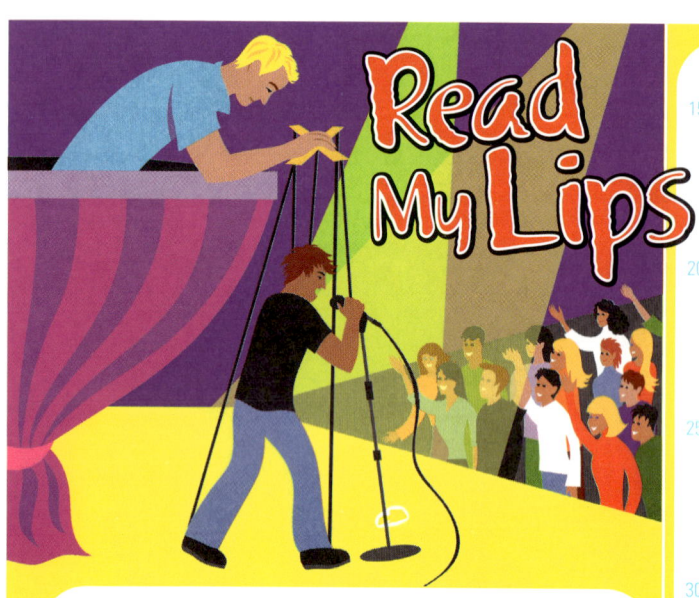

Read My Lips

The time has come to see your favorite musical group live in concert. As the lights dim and the music starts, the lead singer opens her mouth to sing, but her lip movements do not match the words you hear. The music stops and there is a commotion on stage. It becomes obvious that, instead of singing, she intended to simply play a recorded version of her song.

Lip-synching, (pretending to sing to recorded music) can disappoint fans. Some even become ex-fans after attending a lip-synched show. Since 1990 when music sensation Milli Vanilli turned out to be nothing more than actors on stage, lip-synching became the worst-kept secret in the music industry. In the 1990s, angry fans filed lawsuits against groups such as New Kids on the Block, Madonna, Britney Spears, 'N Sync, and the Backstreet Boys. Legislation was proposed demanding that music groups warn concert-goers when pre-recordings are used, but no such law ever went into effect. Secret lip-synching could occur at any "live" performance you attend.

Of course, some fans actually do not mind the use of pre-recordings. Some go to concerts to see the dance moves and enjoy the multi-sensory experience. Since most musicians can't do their dance moves and sing at the same time, these fans are willing to accept canned sounds to get impressive visuals. Most fans, however, feel cheated and resentful when they find out that part of a concert is being lip-synched. The secret slips out, and someone who paid for an expensive concert ticket wishes he had bought a few music videos instead.

The career-damaging potential of secret lip-synching may give performers a strong enough reason not to do it. Christina Aguilera angered fans when she reportedly lip-synched at a concert in New York City in February, 2007. Fans realized that she was using a pre-recording when the band experienced some technical difficulties and her voice came on when she wasn't singing. Ashlee Simpson was caught using a pre-recording on a live American TV show in October, 2004. When words for a different song came on when she began to sing, Simpson became flustered and awkwardly hopped off stage. These scandals have hurt their careers.

2. Answer these questions about the reading.

1. The passage mentions some attitudes of fans who are tolerant of lip-synching and some of those who are not tolerant. If one of the following statements is mentioned in the reading as a tolerant attitude, write "T" next to it. If it is mentioned as an attitude that is not tolerant, write "NT". Two of the items are not mentioned in the passage and should not be marked in any way.

_____ When you expect a live performance, it's disappointing to hear a pre-recording.

_____ Some musicians get sick and have to lip-synch.

_____ Concerts are not only about singing, they are about the whole experience.

_____ Concert tickets cost a lot of money so live performances are expected.

_____ Musicians cheat their fans when they lip-synch.

_____ Dance moves can be just as exciting to watch as the music.

_____ Musicians need to protect their vocal cords.

100 Unit 10 Keeping Secrets

2. Which of the following can be inferred about Milli Vanilli?
   a. They were not very good entertainers.
   b. They were not very popular.
   c. They were caught lip-synching.
   d. They were bad at lip-synching.

3. Which of the following can be inferred about music videos?
   a. They are easier to find than concert tickets are.
   b. One of them costs about the same as a concert ticket.
   c. They do not contain any lip-synching.
   d. One of them costs less than a concert ticket.

B ▶ Listen.

Listen to a conversation about lip-synching. You may take notes as you listen. Then answer the questions.

1. Why does the man talk about lip-synching?
   a. He wants to explain to the woman what it is.
   b. He is dissatisfied with a concert in which the musician was doing it.
   c. He likes musicians who do it.
   d. He wants to see if the woman noticed it at the concert.

2. Why does the woman mention where the man was sitting?
   a. To express doubt about his lip-synching claims
   b. To explain why she enjoyed the concert more than he did
   c. To point out that he paid too much for his ticket
   d. To explain why she could see him but he couldn't see her

3. What does the man want musicians to do?
   a. To stop using pre-recorded material at concerts
   b. To stop lip-synching at concerts
   c. To stop keeping the secret about lip-synching from the fans
   d. To do less dancing and more singing

C ▶ Personal interpretation.

Imagine you are a singer and you have a bad cold. Would you sing live and risk hurting your vocal cords or lip-synch to a pre-recording of your voice in order to save your voice? In your notebook, explain what you would do and why. Be prepared to read your written work aloud to the class.

D ▶ Independent speaking.

Set a timer for 45 seconds or have a classmate time you. Within that short time, give a spoken response to the following prompt. You will have 15 seconds to prepare your response.

> Entertainers are in the business of presenting images. To do so, they may have to keep secrets from their audiences. Which kinds of secrets are acceptable for them to keep, and which are not?

11 Sleeping and Dreaming

READING AND SPEAKING

A ▶ Warm up. Discuss the questions with a partner.

1. How many hours of sleep do you usually get each night?
2. Do you sleep soundly at night? Why or why not?
3. How often do you remember your dreams?

B ▶ Read. Read the article on page 103 and answer the questions.

1. How many famous people's dreams are discussed in the article? _____
2. Which of the following is *not* mentioned in the article? Circle the answer.
   a. a dream that resulted in a novel
   b. a dream that resulted in a painting
   c. a dream that resulted in a song
   d. a dream that seemed to hint at future events
3. According to the article, what should you do after you wake up in the morning if you want to remember your dreams? _____

C ▶ Read again. Underline the cause and effect words from the Skill Focus box in the article. Then write the results of the dreams in the chart.

Dreams (Causes)	Results (Effects)
Paul McCartney's dream	
Mary Shelley's dream	
Kurosawa's dream	
Kekule's dream	

Skill Focus: Cause and Effect

A cause is something that makes another thing happen. An effect is an outcome or a consequence. Words that might alert you to a cause-and-effect relationship in a sentence include: *a/the result of, because, because of, due to, lead to, result in, result from,* and *so*:

Mary Shelley's book, *Frankenstein* was the result of a dream.
A dream resulted in Mary Shelley's book, *Frankenstein*.
A dream led to Mary Shelley's book, *Frankenstein*.
Frankenstein was written as a result of a dream.
The discovery was made because of a dream.
The discovery was made due to a dream.

D ▶ Discuss. Discuss the questions in a small group.

1. What other famous dreams or dreamers do you know about?
2. Have you or has anyone you know ever had a dream about something that happened later—a dream predicting the future?

102   Unit 11   Sleeping and Dreaming

Meaningful Dreams

Many people believe that we can turn to our dreams for **guidance** or that our dreams can **reveal** future events or provide warnings. There are accounts of **significant** or meaningful dreams from all over the world. Some dreams have been passed down for generations through the **scriptures** of religious traditions. Dreams have resulted in famous artistic works, and some major scientific discoveries may be due, in part, to dreams.

There are many stories of artists, musicians, writers, and scientists who were **inspired** by dreams. Paul McCartney, of the Beatles, awoke from a dream with a tune in his head, so he sat down and wrote the hit song, "Yesterday." Mary Shelley's book *Frankenstein* was the result of a dream. Japanese filmmaker Kurosawa said that dreams he'd had throughout his life inspired his film, "Dreams." While German scientist Friedrich Kekule was trying to understand the arrangement of hydrogen and carbon atoms in benzene, he dreamed of a snake, biting its own tail, whirling in a circle. His dream led to the discovery of one of the most important structures in **organic chemistry**—a structure now known as the benzene ring.

In the days before his death, Abraham Lincoln reported a strange dream. He told his wife and friends that he dreamed he heard people crying, and he followed the sound to the East Room of the White House. There he found a covered corpse, guarded by soldiers, and a crowd of people **grieving**. He asked who was dead, and one of the soldiers told him the president had been **assassinated**. Many people believe that this dream was a **premonition**—a hint or clue about Lincoln's own assassination soon to follow. Some believe that Lincoln had this dream because somehow his subconscious knew the events to come.

Can *your* dreams give you ideas or solve your problems? Can they give you information about the future? In order to find out, it's necessary to remember your dreams. Put a notebook and pencil near your bed, and write down your dreams every night for a few weeks. If you do this, you'll see whether there's a pattern to your dreams. After you wake up in the morning, lie in bed a few minutes and try to remember your dreams. If you jump up and start your day immediately, you'll probably forget them. Try thinking about a problem before you fall asleep at night. If you do this for several nights, you might discover that you are attempting to solve the problem in your dreams. If you're lucky, you might even find a solution.

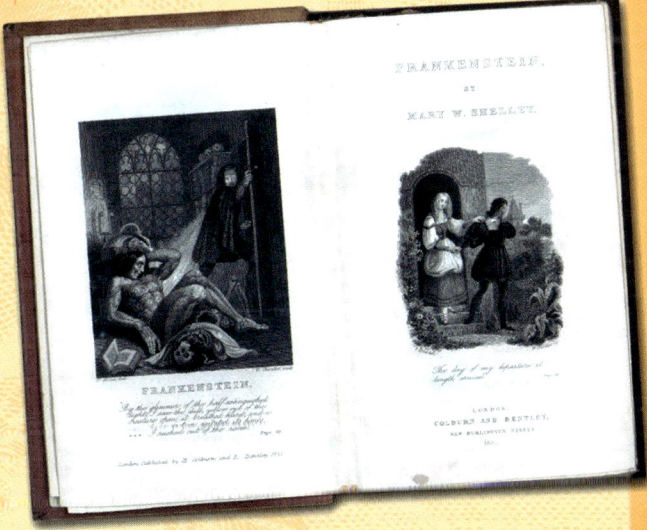

The book *Frankenstein* was inspired by a dream.

LISTENING

E ▶ Listen. Listen to each sentence, followed by a repetition of one clause from the sentence. Does the clause contain a cause or an effect? Write C (cause) or E (effect).

1. _____   2. _____   3. _____   4. _____   5. _____

ACTIVATING GRAMMAR

Future Real Conditional

Conditional sentences express cause and effect. We use the future real conditional to talk about possible actions, situations, or events in the future, and the results of those actions, situations, or events. We use the simple present in the *if* clause and *will / may / might* + verb in the main clause.

If you **write** down your dreams every night, you**'ll see** if there's a pattern to your dreams.
If you **jump** out of bed and start your day immediately, you**'ll** probably **forget** your dreams.
If you **think** about your problems before falling asleep, you **might find** a solution in your dreams.

* *See page 135 for additional grammar practice.*

A ▶ Practice. Complete the future real conditionals with your own ideas. Be sure to use *may* (*not*), *might* (*not*), or *will* (*not*) in the main clause.

1. If you don't get enough sleep tonight, _____.
2. If you drink coffee before bed, _____.
3. _____, you might sleep during your flight tomorrow.
4. _____, I'll wake up early tomorrow.
5. If I can't sleep tonight, _____.
6. _____ I'll probably have stressful dreams tonight.
7. If my alarm doesn't go off in the morning, _____.

104 Unit 11 Sleeping and Dreaming

B ▶ Listen. Listen to the following sentences. Then check (✓) True or False.

	True	False
1. The speaker has an appointment with his doctor.	☐	☐
2. The listener wants the speaker to go to bed soon.	☐	☐
3. He isn't getting enough sleep.	☐	☐
4. The speaker doesn't think the listener is sleeping well.	☐	☐
5. The speaker will take care of the baby the next time she cries tonight.	☐	☐

VOCABULARY

A ▶ Practice. Match the words and their meanings.

1. ___ assassinate
2. ___ grieve
3. ___ guidance
4. ___ inspire
5. ___ organic chemistry
6. ___ premonition
7. ___ reveal
8. ___ scripture
9. ___ significant

a. advice about doing something
b. a branch of chemistry that deals with carbon compounds
c. to make known; to display, to show
d. texts from the major religious traditions of the world
e. to feel sorrow or deep sadness
f. a sense of future danger or evil
g. important
h. to influence or to cause
i. to kill a famous or well-known person, usually for political reasons

B ▶ Discuss. Discuss the following questions with a partner.

1. Other than your parents, who was a significant person in your childhood?
2. Can you think of an event, person, or thing that inspired you to create, write, or do something?
3. Do you believe that dreams can reveal the future? Can they reveal solutions to problems or provide guidance?
4. Have you ever had a premonition in a dream or in your waking life? Do you know anyone who has had one?

LISTENING   I wonder what it means

A ▶ Discuss. Look at the three pictures representing different people's dreams. Predict what might happen next. Write your predictions.

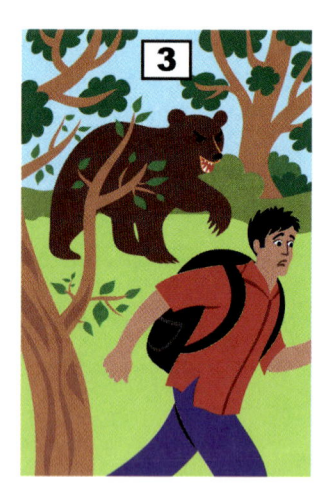

1. _____   2. _____   3. _____

B ▶ Listen. Check (✓) how close your prediction was to what really happened.

	Partially correct	Completely wrong
1. Beach Dream	....	....
2. House Dream	....	....
3. Forest Dream	....	....

C ▶ Listen again. Which of the following inferences could you make based on each conversation? Write the letter on the line.

Conversation 1: _____

Conversation 2: _____

Conversation 3: _____

  a. The woman believes that dreams are just a replay of the day's activities. Images of the day go through our minds in dreams.
  b. The woman believes dreams symbolize conflicts in the dreamer's own mind or psyche or subconscious.
  c. The woman believes the subconscious guides people in their dreams.

Skill Focus — Making Inferences
We often guess, or infer, additional information based on information that we actually hear. Often, we can logically "fill in" details based on information the speaker gives, or based on body language or tone of voice. Inferences may be accurate or inaccurate.

106   Unit 11   Sleeping and Dreaming

D ▶ Pair work. Check (✓) the topics you can remember dreaming about. Describe a dream you can remember to your partner. Talk about what your dreams might have meant.

Dream and nightmare topics		
☐ water or waves	☐ death or dead people	☐ an animal
☐ flying	☐ being chased by someone or something	☐ war or violence
☐ traveling	☐ a house or building	☐ other

CONVERSATION STRATEGY   Showing That You Are Paying Attention

🎧 **A ▶ Pair work.** Circle the best word to complete each conversation. Listen and check your answers. Then practice the conversations with a partner.

These are expressions that you can use to show that you are following a speaker:
* Hmm.   * Really?
* Huh.

These expressions indicate that you're following and imply that you agree with the speaker:
* Yeah.   * Mm-hmm.
* Right.   * Uh-huh.

1. **A:** I had a terrible dream last night. It woke me up.
   B: _____ (Huh. / Right.) I heard you.
   A: I dreamed people were chasing me. I thought they were trying to kill me. You were with them.
   B: _____ (Really? / Yeah.)
   A: Yes. I ran into a house, and I went into the bathroom to hide. I heard someone follow me into the house. I knew it was you.
   B: _____ (Right. / Hmm.)

2. **A:** Last night, I dreamed my cat could talk.
   B: _____ (Hmm. / Yeah.)
   A: She looked at me and said, "You will never know me as well as I know you."
   B: _____ (Huh. / Right.)
   A: And what she said is probably true. I think cats know their owners very well.
   B: _____ (Mm-hmm. / Hmm.) They do.
   A: Anyway, I don't remember what else my cat said, but we had a long, serious conversation. I know you'll say this dream probably symbolized something.
   B: _____ (Uh-huh. / Huh.) I think it does.

> **Skill Focus**
> **Showing That You Are Paying Attention**
> It's natural to show that you are following or paying attention to what a speaker is saying. Sometimes this is best done with a short word or phrase—perhaps when you don't want to interrupt, or perhaps when you don't want to encourage the speaker to continue talking by giving longer responses.

B ▶ Role-play. Work with a partner. Be sure it's not the same partner you had in Listening Activity D. Tell each other your dreams and discuss their meanings. As you talk, use the target words from Activity A.

WRITING   Writing about Cause and Effect

A ▶ Study it. Study the two paragraphs about sleep deprivation on page 109.

1. Underline the topic sentence in each paragraph.
2. Which paragraph is about cause, and which is about effect?

B ▶ Write it.

1. Choose a problem to write about. Use a topic below, or choose your own.

   Possible topics:
   - crime
   - climate change
   - diabetes (or another illness)
   - noise pollution
   - stress
   - unhealthy lifestyles

2. Write the problem on the line. Then list possible causes and possible effects of the problem in the chart.

   Problem: _____

Causes	Effects

3. Write one paragraph describing causes of the problem and one paragraph describing effects of the problem. Try to use at least one conditional sentence.

> **Skill Focus: Writing about Cause and Effect**
> When writers want to analyze or discuss a problem, they often organize their writing in a way that focuses on causes and effects. Often they will devote one paragraph or section to discussing causes or possible causes and another paragraph or section to discussing effects or possible effects. The topic sentence in each paragraph should indicate whether the paragraph is about causes or effects of the specific problem, or both.

> **TIP: Symptoms**
> When discussing an illness or disease, the effects on the physical body are called "symptoms."

Unit 11   Sleeping and Dreaming

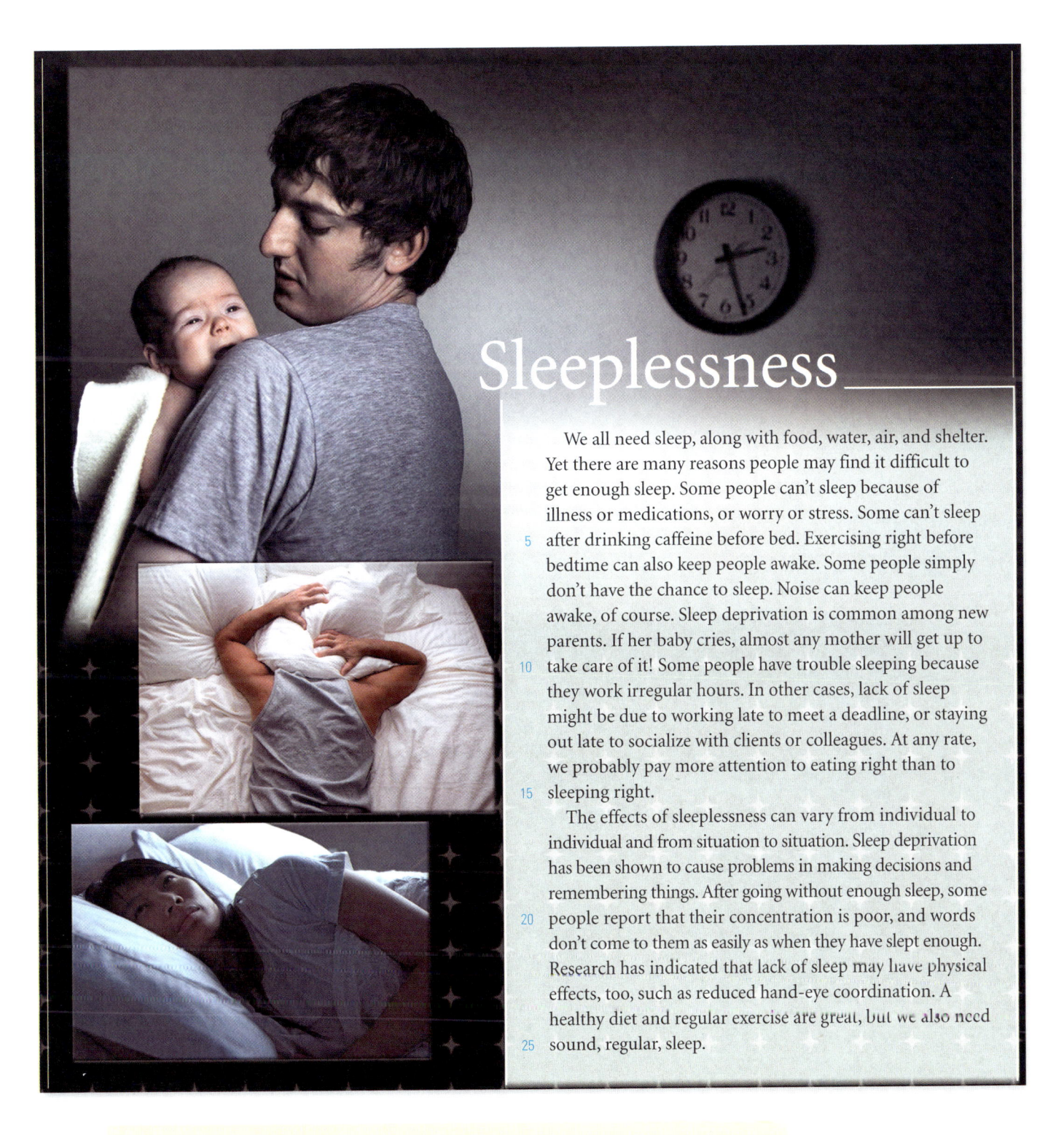

Sleeplessness

We all need sleep, along with food, water, air, and shelter. Yet there are many reasons people may find it difficult to get enough sleep. Some people can't sleep because of illness or medications, or worry or stress. Some can't sleep after drinking caffeine before bed. Exercising right before bedtime can also keep people awake. Some people simply don't have the chance to sleep. Noise can keep people awake, of course. Sleep deprivation is common among new parents. If her baby cries, almost any mother will get up to take care of it! Some people have trouble sleeping because they work irregular hours. In other cases, lack of sleep might be due to working late to meet a deadline, or staying out late to socialize with clients or colleagues. At any rate, we probably pay more attention to eating right than to sleeping right.

The effects of sleeplessness can vary from individual to individual and from situation to situation. Sleep deprivation has been shown to cause problems in making decisions and remembering things. After going without enough sleep, some people report that their concentration is poor, and words don't come to them as easily as when they have slept enough. Research has indicated that lack of sleep may have physical effects, too, such as reduced hand-eye coordination. A healthy diet and regular exercise are great, but we also need sound, regular, sleep.

Editing Checklist

- Did you write one paragraph about the cause of a problem?
- Did you write another paragraph about effects of the problem?
- Did each paragraph have a topic sentence?
- Were there supporting sentences and details for the topic sentences?
- Did your paragraph include at least one conditional sentence?

PUT IT TO THE TEST

A ▶ Read.

1. Read the article. Then answer the questions that follow.

Dreaming the Future

One night, a woman woke up from a dream at precisely 9:03 pm. In her dream she saw her father die outside a hospital in Glasgow. Two months later at exactly 9:03, her father died in the same spot she had seen in her dream. Her dream turned out to be a premonition.

In cultural traditions throughout the world, premonition dreams have long been accepted as real and significant. They were recorded on clay tablets by the ancient Assyrians and Babylonians, and were taken very seriously in classical Egypt, Greece, and Rome. Modern research shows that premonition dreams are more common among women than among men. The future events usually involve people close to the dreamer.

The events foretold in premonition dreams may not occur until several weeks after the dream. Some dreamers even appear to keep to a regular schedule. Barbara Garwell, a woman who consistently has premonition dreams, claims that 21 days after she dreams about an event, it comes true. For example, in September of 1981, she dreamed that a group of dignitaries from the Middle East were assassinated while sitting in stadium seats. On October 6, twenty-one days after her dream, the President of Egypt, Anwar Sadat, was assassinated along with seven other people while watching a parade from stadium-like seats in Cairo.

Premonition dreams have apparently evolved to suit modern cultures. In the past, one's ancestors might have been the source of a prediction in a dream. Now, that role might be played by an electronic gadget. One researcher who has classified premonition dreams has defined a "media announcement type" category. In this type of dream, the person sees information about a future event from some type of media, such as a newspaper or radio or TV show. According to one study, dreams like this are particularly accurate.

Very few scientists, however, think dreams can truly predict the future. It is illogical, and therefore unscientific, to think that an effect (knowledge of an event) can appear before its cause (the event). Some skeptics say that so-called premonitions are really just inferences or educated guesses about what might happen. Other critics believe that any similarity between a dream and a real-life event is only a coincidence.

2. Answer these questions about the reading.

1. Which of the following best expresses the essential information in the highlighted sentence? *Incorrect* answer choices change the meaning in important ways or leave out essential information.
   a. Scientists have been unable to identify the causes of dreams.
   b. Premonition dreamers fail to think about causes and effects.
   c. Scientists believe we should think more about the effects of dreams.
   d. It does not make sense to think that an effect can precede its cause.

2. The word traditions in the passage is closest in meaning to _____.
   a. populations
   b. economies
   c. customs
   d. religions

3. The word ancestors in the passage is closest in meaning to _____.
   a. ancient people
   b. older relatives
   c. traditional deities
   d. respected leaders

B ▶ Listen.

Listen to a lecture on the science of dreams. You may take notes as you listen. Then answer the questions.

1. What is the main topic of the lecture?
   a. Theories about dreams
   b. Sigmund Freud
   c. Premonition dreams
   d. Psychological theories

2. Listen again to two passages from the lecture. Answer the question you hear after each passage.

   1. a. It is not supported by dream research.
      b. It has introduced science into the study of dreams.
      c. It explains the current popularity of dream research.
      d. It has led to a lot of disagreement among dream researchers.

   2. a. To point out that dreams have inspired great literature
      b. To emphasize that the brain is responsible for the order in dream images
      c. To highlight our ability to consciously make dreams say what we want them to say
      d. To imply that no one can accurately recall the events in a dream

C ▶ Personal interpretation.

Do you think dreams can predict the future? Have you ever dreamed about something that happened later? If so, tell about it. Prepare a two-minute spoken response to these questions.

D ▶ Integrated writing.

Write a response of about 175 words to the following prompt. Use specific reasons and examples to support your response. You have 20 minutes to plan and write your response.

> Summarize the points made in the lecture, being sure to specifically explain how they strengthen points made in the reading passage.

He loved to dream about the future. But never more than 11 minutes into the future.

Unit 11 Sleeping and Dreaming 111

12 Movies

READING AND SPEAKING

A ▶ Warm up. Look at the photos representing different types of movies. Discuss them with a partner.

1. What type of movie does each photo represent? What are some other types?
2. What is a good movie you've seen lately? Why did you like it?

B ▶ Read. Read the web page on page 113 and answer the questions.

Who says that s/he . . .	Name	Job
1. wears a headset?		
2. loves her work?		
3. reads a script many times?		
4. hit some raw chicken breasts?		
5. likes the people he works with?		
6. doesn't have to do anything dangerous?		

C ▶ Read again. How interesting are the jobs you listed in Activity B? Rank them from 1 to 6. (1 is most interesting and 6 is least interesting.) Then explain your rankings to a partner.

1. ____   4. ____
2. ____   5. ____
3. ____   6. ____

Skill Focus: Relating to Content as You Read
You will remember and understand information better if you can relate it to personal experience or feelings. As you read the web page about careers in the movie industry, ask yourself whether you would like each career, whether you have any experience related to it, and whether it has any connection to any of your interests.

112   Unit 12   Movies

What Do They Do?

When you think about the people involved in making a movie, actors, producers, and directors might come to mind. But there are many others who work hard to make a movie happen. Here are some people who work behind the scenes:

Luz Ramirez: I'm an art director. I work with the director on all the visual **aspects** of a movie. I manage the people who work on the set – you know the background and furniture and things like that. Also people who work on props – the smaller things the actors carry or use on stage, and costumes. I love my work. The right sets and costumes
5 are the things that allow the actors to come alive. I read the **script** many times to make sure that I'm creating the right environment for the movie.

Artie Slocum: I'm a floor manager. The director can't be everywhere at once. I wear a **headset** so the director and technical director can speak to me during filming. I communicate their directions to the **cast** and **crew** using hand signals. I really enjoy my job. I feel like
10 I'm a bridge between the thoughts of the director and the action on the set.

Mark Peterson: Some people think a stand-in is a stuntperson. Actually, the jobs aren't the same. I don't have to do anything dangerous. I have the same **build** and coloring as many male celebrities. So when the lighting crew is trying to set up the right light for a shot, I stand in the place where the celebrity will be. When the camera operators need to
15 decide on camera **angles**, or when a director wants to see how the scene would look with the actor in a different position, I **fill in**. I like my job, and I like the people I work with.

Amy Loy: I'm a Foley artist. I have the best job in the world! I work in a room called a sound stage. It's protected from outside noise. Work is like play to me. I use all kinds of things to create sound effects – of rain, of footsteps, of doors opening . . . any sounds
20 I don't have a recording of. Once, to make the sound of men **punching** each other, I hit some raw chicken breasts. I put the chicken breasts between pieces of plastic wrap first so that when I was done I could take them home and cook them!

Do any of these careers appeal to you? Click on the link below! Fun Careers in Film

D ▶ Discuss. Discuss these questions in a small group.
1. Which of the following qualities describe you? What other qualities describe you?
   creative   communicative   curious   patient
2. Which of these qualities do you think describe the people in the article? What other qualities should the people have? Why?
3. Is there anyone in the film industry that you admire? Explain.

LISTENING

Listen to the children, and predict which jobs they might be good at or interested in when they grow up. Match the letter of the occupation with the number of the speaker.

____ 1.   ____ 3.   a. art director   c. stand-in
____ 2.   ____ 4.   b. floor manager   d. Foley artist

ACTIVATING GRAMMAR

Reported Speech

Reported speech involves one person telling what another said. In reported speech, the reporting verb (*say*, *tell*, *mention*, etc.) is usually in the simple past. We usually change the verb from the direct speech to a past form.

Direct Speech	Reported Speech
"I have a headache."	Ed **said (that)** he **had** a headache.
"I'm looking for my keys."	Aaron **said (that)** he **was looking** for his keys.

The change to a past form of the verb from the direct speech is optional when it refers to an action, state, or situation that is still true.

Direct Speech	Reported Speech
"I love my class."	Tami **said (that)** she **loves** her work.
"I have a cat."	Andy **told** me **(that)** he **has** a cat.

When the reporting verb is in the simple present, the verb from the direct speech does not change. (When we report on something we read, we often use the simple present. The direct speech sentences below are from the reading on page 113. Luz did not say she loved her work in a past encounter. In a sense, she is still saying it now since it is in written form, so the reported speech uses the simple present.)

Direct Speech	Reported Speech
"I love my work."	Luz **says (that)** she **loves** her work.
"Work is like play to me."	Amy **says (that)** work **is** like play to her.

See page 135 for additional grammar practice.

A ▶ Read. What does this critic say about the movie *Casino Royale*? Change the numbered sentences to reported speech.

The New James Bond in *Casino Royale*

(1) *Casino Royale* is a huge success. (2) Daniel Craig is fantastic as the new James Bond. (3) The story is action-packed, and the special effects are incredible. (4) The script is well-written, and the music is great. (5) I predict that we'll see Craig in many more James Bond movies.

1. This critic says that Casino Royale is a huge success.
2. _____
3. _____
4. _____
5. _____

B ▶ Pair work. Ask a partner the questions below. Then use reported speech to write what your partner said. Change the reporting verb to the simple past. Use the simple present verb from the direct speech (the question) if the information is still true.

Example: **A:** What's your favorite movie?

B: My favorite movie is *Star Wars*.

She said that her favorite movie is *Star Wars*.

1. What's your favorite movie?
2. How many movies do you go to or rent each month?
3. Do you want to see any movies that are playing right now?

VOCABULARY

A ▶ Practice. Complete the sentences with the words from the box.

angles	build	crew	headset
aspects	cast	fill in	punching

1. The technical _____ went out for lunch, but the _____ had to stay and practice their scenes.
2. She doesn't really have the right _____ for a model, but our camera operator can make her look taller by shooting from certain _____.
3. He's worked here a long time and understands all the different _____ of our business. He can _____ for anyone on our team.
4. Her two little girls were _____ each other and shouting, but she didn't hear them because she was listening to music on her _____.

B ▶ Listen. Listen to these co-workers. Check (✓) True or False for each statement.

                                                                                                                       True   **False**

1. The man said that he saw people shooting a movie in the park. ☐ ☐
2. The man recognized two of the cast members. ☐ ☐
3. The woman said she was wearing a headset on her way to work. ☐ ☐
4. The man said that two actors seemed to be punching each other. ☐ ☐
5. The woman said the stand-ins couldn't fill in for the actors. ☐ ☐
6. The man says that he doesn't know about many aspects of filmmaking. ☐ ☐

LISTENING   What did you say?

A ▶ Discuss. Discuss these topics in a small group.
1. a celebrity you've met
2. a celebrity you've seen in public but didn't talk to
3. a film you've seen being made
4. the actor you think is the most talented

🎧 **B ▶ Listen.** Listen to three friends talking. Check (✓) the name of the person who originally made each statement.

Quote	Nadia	Alicia	David
1. "Gael Garcia Bernal is going to shoot a new movie near the university."	☐	☐	☐
2. "Gael Garcia Bernal is an incredible actor!"	☐	☐	☐
3. "I didn't make it up."	☐	☐	☐
4. "I don't know the story, but I'm confident it will be good."	☐	☐	☐
5. "He was outstanding in his last three movies."	☐	☐	☐
6. "Being nominated for an award doesn't make Bernal a better actor."	☐	☐	☐

🎧 **C ▶ Listen again.** Restate the information from Activity B using a verb from the box. More than one choice is possible.

Skill Focus — Restating Information
Sometimes we need to restate information we have heard. To do this, we use reported speech. Although we do not change the meaning of someone's words when we report their speech, we can choose the reporting verb. While *say* and *tell* are common reporting verbs, other verbs are more specific. Listening to the speaker's tone of voice and choice of words can help us choose the best verb.

argue	claim	emphasize
exclaim	insist	suggest

1. David claimed that Gael Garcia Bernal was going to shoot a new movie near the university.
2. _____
3. _____
4. _____
5. _____
6. _____

116   Unit 12   Movies

D ▸ Pair work. Interview a partner about his or her favorite actor. Then report the information to the class.

1. Who is your favorite actor? _____
2. Which film is the actor's best work? _____
3. Why do you like this actor? _____

CONVERSATION STRATEGY Speculating

A ▸ Pair work. Complete the conversations with expressions from the box. Listen and check your answers. Then practice with a partner.

* **I heard (that)** he posted it on YouTube.
* **Someone told me (that)** you were making a movie.
* **I think (that)** I'll look for it tonight.
* **I haven't heard about** anyone who's made a lot of money from an amateur video.
* **Didn't someone say (that)** shooting a video and posting it on YouTube is a better way to get started in movies than going to film school?

A: Hey, _____
B: No. Not me. My brother. It's a great film. You should watch it. He was his own actor, his own cameraman, his own crew, his own Foley artist. The guy is amazing.
A: Wow. Can I get a copy to watch?
B: I don't think you'll need to. _____.
A: Really? That's great. Then I can watch it on my computer. _____ Do you want to come over?
B: Sure. I'd like to see what else is new on YouTube, too.
A: _____
_____
B: Well, yeah, my brother said that.
A: No, I mean someone famous.
B: Oh. Well, I believe it. I think film school could be a waste of time and money.
A: Hmm. I'm not sure about that. I mean, _____.

B ▸ Role-play. Work with a partner. Think about something you've heard recently. Use one of the ideas below or your own idea. Write a short dialogue, using some of the target language from Activity A. Practice your dialogue until you can act it out without reading. Role-play the conversation for your class.

1. a rumor or gossip about a celebrity or public figure
2. something positive you've heard about a friend or classmate

Unit 12 Movies **117**

WRITING Using Introductory Clauses

A ▶ Study it.

1. Read the movie review on page 119 and underline the clauses beginning with *although*, *even though*, and *while*.

2. What are three things about the movie that the reviewer dislikes or criticizes?

   1. _____
   2. _____
   3. _____

> **Skill Focus**
>
> **Introductory Clauses with *although*, *even though*, and *while***
>
> Sometimes when giving an opinion, a writer will start with a comment or information that seems to support a contrary view. Clauses beginning with *Although . . .*, *Even though . . .*, and *While . . .* are often used in these instances. The ideas in these clauses are not the writer's focus—the main point comes in the following part of the sentence.

3. What are three things about the movie that the reviewer likes or praises?

   1. _____
   2. _____
   3. _____

4. Is the review generally positive or negative?

B ▶ Write it. Write a review of a movie you have seen recently.

1. Choose a movie that you have a strong positive or a strong negative opinion about.

2. List at least three things you liked or disliked about the movie.

   _____
   _____
   _____

3. Think of clauses beginning with *although*, *even though*, and *while* that could introduce the things you listed in Item 2.

4. Write your review. Include a topic sentence that gives the main idea – your overall opinion about the movie. Support your topic sentence with information including the things you listed in Item 2. Introduce each thing you listed in Item 2 with a clause beginning with *although*, *even though*, or *while*.

118 Unit 12 Movies

Fearless

Actor Jet Li and choreographer Woo-ping Yuen have given the public another amazing martial arts epic movie. Even people who are not martial arts fans will not want to miss this one. Although the story, based on the life of Huo Yuanjia, moves slowly at times, the choreography is brilliant, and the action is fast. Woo-ping Yuen's work in this movie is the best of his career. And while the movie is full of violence, the fight scenes are wonderful. Jet Li performs beautifully. Even though the script is weak, his acting is good. He is convincing in his role of Huo Yuanjia, who founded the Jin Wu Sports Federation. In the film, when Huo Yuanjia is a boy, his father does not want him to fight, but this only makes him more determined to prove himself. Seeking fame and glory leads to his downfall, and Huo Yuanjia must find honor and humility. To say much more about the main character would give away the plot of the story. But what about the other characters? Although their acting is good, it isn't as wonderful as Jet Li's. Betty Sun, who plays Moon, isn't strong in her role. But she is very pretty. Despite its few weaknesses, this is an excellent movie. Jet Li has said that this is his last big martial arts epic. I hope he changes his mind, but if he doesn't, this is a great movie for him to end with. I highly recommend it.

Editing Checklist

- Did you include a topic sentence that clearly gives your overall opinion about the movie?
- Did you include at least three supporting examples or ideas?
- Did you use *although*, *even though*, and *while*?

Unit 12   Movies   119

PUT IT TO THE TEST

A ▶ Read.

1. Read the article. Then answer the questions that follow.

Vlogging Your Way to Fame

You can now make it big in the movies without ever leaving your living room. All you need is a video camera, a computer, and YouTube. Since the video-sharing website was founded in 2005, it has been a huge success. During a typical 24-hour period, more than 100 million viewings and 65,000 submissions of new videos take place at the YouTube site (according to a July 16, 2006 survey). Now, the vloggers (people who share their homemade video clips) are becoming celebrities. Just ask Brookers, LisaNova, and even Lonelygirl15. Brookers, also known as Brooke Brodock, is considered the first person to have moved from YouTube directly to mainstream media. She started posting her short comedic videos on YouTube in September 2005, and only nine months later she signed a contract with a production company. Brooke directs, edits, and performs in all her home-based videos. All together, her videos have had more than 29 million hits, with her most popular video, "CRAZED NUMA FAN!!!!" exceeding 5.5 million hits.

Like Brookers, Lisa Donovan (YouTube name: LisaNova) has become a star by producing short comedy films and posting them on YouTube. After a few hundred thousand people viewed the first comedy skit she posted, she and some friends put up more, and she is now YouTube's 14th most popular channel, with over 28,000 subscribers. Lisa recently signed a contract to appear as a member on a hit comedy show, *MADtv*.

The idea that anyone can become a celebrity attracts people to YouTube. Hollywood and big TV networks don't have any control over the celebrity prospects of these ordinary people. Vloggers are proving that they can make it on their own. In fact, when Lonelygirl15, a vlogger named Bree, was discovered to actually be actress Jessica Rose, her fan base dropped significantly. Many let her know that YouTube is for ordinary people and not for Hollywood stars.

Source: Accessed May 2007 at http://en.wikipedia.org/wiki/YouTube#Fame-beyond-YouTube

2. Answer the questions about the reading.

1. An introductory sentence for a brief summary of the passage is provided below. Complete the summary by selecting the THREE answer choices that express the most important ideas in the passage. Some sentences do not belong in the summary because they express ideas that are not presented in the passage or are minor ideas in the passage.

   Ordinary people can become famous by posting homemade videos to the YouTube website.

   a. Vloggers post short videos, many of which are funny, based on their own experiences or interests.
   b. Many people log on to YouTube every day.
   c. YouTube users reject professional actors as vloggers because the site is for ordinary people.
   d. Brooke Brodock and Lisa Donovan, who posted comedy videos, are some of the vloggers who have made it big.
   e. CRAZED NUMA FAN!!!! is one video that made Brooke Brodock a star.
   f. Lisa Donovan's channel is the 14th most popular channel on YouTube.

2. The word *it* in the passage refers to _____.
   a. the Internet
   b. the World Wide Web
   c. YouTube
   d. a Website

3. The word more in the passage refers to _____.
   a. skits
   b. videos
   c. friends
   d. vloggers

B ▶ Listen.

Listen to part of a conversation between two friends. You may take notes as you listen. Then answer the questions.

1. What is the man's son doing?
   a. Making videos to put on YouTube
   b. Spending too much time on YouTube
   c. Watching too much TV
   d. Spending too much time on e-mail

2. According to the woman, vloggers make videos that are all _____.
   a. short
   b. funny
   c. bad
   d. expensive

3. What can be inferred about the man?
   a. He doesn't know much about using the Internet.
   b. He has trouble understanding how computers work.
   c. He doesn't want to get involved in his son's life.
   d. He wants to ban his son from watching YouTube.

C ▶ Personal interpretation.

Try to imagine the entertainment business 10 years in the future. In what ways might video-sharing Websites, such as YouTube, change the movie and TV industry? Prepare a two-minute spoken response to this question.

D ▶ Integrated speaking.

Prepare a response to the following question. You will have 20 seconds to prepare and 60 seconds to give your response.

> In the listening section, two people discuss possible solutions to the man's problem. Describe the problem. Then state which of the two solutions you prefer and explain why.

GRAMMAR EXPANSION ACTIVITIES

UNIT 1 Questions in the Simple Present and Simple Past

A ▶ Complete the sentences with the simple present or the simple past forms of the verbs in the box. You will use some verbs more than once. Then write answers to the questions.

be	go	come	do	have	rent	watch

1. _____ you interested in the lives of celebrities these days?
   _____

2. In elementary school, who _____ your favorite actor or TV character?
   _____

3. Last week, _____ you _____ to a movie or _____ a DVD?
   _____

4. _____ any famous actors or singers _____ from your hometown?
   _____

5. How often _____ you _____ TV online?
   _____

6. Who _____ your favorite athletes when you were a child?
   _____

7. What _____ the best book you read last year?
   _____

8. _____ you _____ a job right now?
   _____

B ▶ Imagine you (A) are interviewing an actor (B) about a movie he made recently. Read his answers. Write a possible question for each answer.

Example: *Did you like the people you worked with?*

Well, I liked most of them, but I didn't like the director.

1. **A:** _____
   B: It took about six months to film the movie. We finished on schedule.

2. **A:** _____
   B: We worked about seven hours a day. It was very difficult.

3. **A:** _____
   B: Yes. I have an assistant named Bruce. He did a lot of work for this movie.

4. **A:** _____
   B: We made the movie in California.

5. **A:** _____
   B: Yes, I'm really happy with the movie. I think it's one of my best.

UNIT 2 The Simple Present, Present Continuous, Simple Past, and the Past Continuous

A ▶ Complete the conversation. Use the simple present or the present continuous.

A: Elizabeth, you _____ (wear) too much perfume! It _____ (be) *really* strong.
　　　　　　　　　　　1　　　　　　　　　　　　　　　　　　2

B: Oh, sorry. Thanks for telling me. I _____ (no / have) any sense of smell.
　　　　　　　　　　　　　　　　　　　　　　3

　　I never _____ (know) how much perfume to use.
　　　　　　　　4

A: Really? You can't smell anything at all?

B: No. Right now I _____ (date) a man who can't believe it, either. We _____ (take) a
　　　　　　　　　　　5　　　　　　　　　　　　　　　　　　　　　　　　　　　　　　　　6

　　cooking class together. He _____ always _____ (tell) me how great the food smells.
　　　　　　　　　　　　　　　　　00　　　　　　　　　　7

A: Can you taste the food?

B: Yes, but I _____ (no / know) if I can taste as strongly as other people. Taste and smell
　　　　　　　　8

　　_____ (be) connected, you know.
　　　　9

A: Yeah. That's too bad.

B: Well, I _____ still _____ (live) with my mother, and she's a great cook.
　　　　　　　00　　　　　　　10

　　_____ you _____ (go) anywhere right now? If you're free, why don't you come over
　　　00　　　　　　　11

　　for dinner? Mom _____ (cook) chicken every Tuesday.
　　　　　　　　　　12

A: OK. Actually, I _____ (be) hungry.
　　　　　　　　　　13

B ▶ Complete the paragraphs. Use the simple past or the past continuous.

Last year, I ___*learned*___ (learn) that I was allergic to cats. One day I _____ (watch) TV
　　1

when my little sister _____ (bring) a cat home. At first, I _____ (like) the cat. But soon I
　　　　　　　　　　　2　　　　　　　　　　　　　　　　　　　　3

_____ (start) to cough and sneeze. My eyes _____ (begin) to water. My sister
　　4　　　　　　　　　　　　　　　　　　　　　　　5

_____ (think) I _____ (cry). I told her I _____ (no / cry). I _____
　　6　　　　　　　　7　　　　　　　　　　　　　　　8　　　　　　　　　　　　　9

(explain) that I was allergic to the cat. Then my *sister* started to cry. She _____ (want) to keep the
　　　10

cat. While she _____ (hold) the cat and _____ (cry), my father _____ (come)
　　　　　　　　11　　　　　　　　　　　　　　　　12　　　　　　　　　　　　　13

home. He said there _____ (be) another little girl outside near our house. The other girl
　　　　　　　　　　14

_____ (cry) too. Our father said the other girl _____ probably still _____
　　15　　　　　　　　　　　　　　　　　　　　　　　00　　　　　　　　　　　　　16

(walk) up and down the street. She _____ (call), "Kitty-kitty-kitty!"
　　　　　　　　　　　　　　　　　17

We _____ (know) the girl was looking for the cat. We all _____ (go) outside to find
　　18　　　　　　　　　　　　　　　　　　　　　　　　　　　　　　　19

the girl. We finally _____ (find) her, and my sister tried to give her the cat. But the cat jumped out
　　　　　　　　　21

of my sister's arms and _____ (get) away. It _____ (run) under a car.
　　　　　　　　　　　　22　　　　　　　　　　　23

Soon both girls _____ (cry) again!
　　　　　　　　　24

UNIT 3 Gerunds and Infinitives

A ▶ Rewrite the sentences. Change the infinitives to gerunds.

1. My friend likes to talk about her relationship problems.
   _____

2. Kim loves to read stories about love and romantic relationships.
   _____

3. Why don't you try to find a romantic partner online?
   _____

4. When did you start to date each other?
   _____

5. Would you prefer to have a quiet boyfriend or girlfriend or someone who is outgoing?
   _____

6. Will Tom and Jen continue to see each other after Tom leaves for college?
   _____

B ▶ Match the sentences on the left with the closest meaning on the right.

1. _____ I stopped eating fast food.   a. I don't eat fast food anymore.
   _____ I stopped to eat fast food.   b. I took time to eat fast food.

2. _____ Can you remember mailing the letter?   a. Please mail the letter.
         Don't forget, OK?
   _____ Can you remember to mail the letter?   b. Do you know if you already mailed the letter?

3. _____ I won't forget taking her to the concert.   a. I have a memory of when I took her to the concert.
   _____ I won't forget to take her to the concert. b. I'll keep my promise. I'll take her to the concert.

Unit 3 Grammar Expansion **125**

UNIT 4 Dependent and Independent Clauses

A ▶ Read the sentences. Write IC (Independent Clause) or DC (Dependent Clause) under each underlined clause.

1. When I graduate, I want to be an archaeologist.
   _____   _____

2. While I was digging in my garden, I found an old necklace.
   _____   _____

3. I had a dream about my father, but I forgot the details.
   _____   _____

4. I'm having trouble in my relationship with my wife, so we're going to see a counselor.
   _____   _____

5. I've never visited a mine, but I'd like to see one.
   _____   _____

6. When the construction workers were digging, they discovered an old cemetery.
   _____   _____

7. While I was in school, I studied archaeology and anthropology.
   _____   _____

B ▶ Complete the sentences with independent clauses.

1. I want to do well in this class, so _____.
2. It looks like it might rain, but _____.
3. While I was coming to class, _____.
4. _____, and he's also famous.
5. _____, but I don't have time.
6. When I finish this class, _____.

126   Unit 4   Grammar Expansion

UNIT 5 Simple Present for Future

Look at Julie's flight itinerary for a trip she's taking next week. Then answer the questions about her plans. Write full sentences. Use the simple present.

Flight Itinerary

Flight out

Tuesday June 17

Departs New York	9:45 A.M.
Arrives Chicago	1:55 P.M.
Departs Chicago	2:30 P.M.
Arrives Clay City	3:55 P.M.

Flight back

Wednesday June 25

Departs Clay City	6:20 A.M.
Arrives Chicago	7:15 A.M.
Departs Chicago	9:20 A.M.
Arrives New York	12:20 P.M.

1. What day does Julie leave?

   _____

2. What day docs she return?

   _____

3. What time does she arrive in Chicago on June 17th?

   _____

4. What time does her flight to Clay City leave from Chicago?

   _____

5. What time does she get back in New York on June 25th?

   _____

6. How much time does she have between flights on the 25th?

   _____

UNIT 6 Quantifiers: *a few*, *few*, *a little*, and *little*

Complete the sentences with *a few*, *a little*, *few*, or *little*. Then check whether the sentence is true or false for you.

1. I'm so busy! I have _____ time to study English.
   ____ True   ____ False

2. I don't speak a lot of English, but I watch _____ movies in English every month.
   ____ True   ____ False

3. I try to learn _____ new English vocabulary words every week.
   ____ True   ____ False

4. Many people speak two languages, and a few speak three. But _____ people speak more than three languages.
   ____ True   ____ False

5. I have _____ trouble remembering new words. I need a study plan.
   ____ True   ____ False

6. I study regularly with _____ of my classmates.
   ____ True   ____ False

7. My sister is good at English. She gives me _____ help with my homework.
   ____ True   ____ False

8. I have _____ chances to speak English, except in class.
   ____ True   ____ False

9. I'd like to travel all over the world. I have big plans, but _____ money!
   ____ True   ____ False

10. I study every day, so I'm making _____ progress.
    ____ True   ____ False

UNIT 7 The Past Perfect and the Simple Past

Combine the two sentences into one sentence. Use the bold words to begin your sentence.

1. He reached his 30th birthday.　　　　　He made three million dollars.
   (happened after)　　　　　　　　　　　(happened before)
   By the time

   By the time he reached his 30th birthday, he had made three million dollars.

   OR

   He had made three million dollars by the time he reached his 30th birthday.

2. It started to snow.　　　　　　　　　　We got to the restaurant.
   (happened first)　　　　　　　　　　　(happened second)
   When

   _____

3. He retired.　　　　　　　　　　　　　He finished writing his novel.
   (happened first)　　　　　　　　　　　(happened second)
   By the time

   _____

4. His finished washing the dishes.　　　　His wife finished putting their son to bed.
   (happened second)　　　　　　　　　　(happened first)
   When

   _____

5. She fell asleep.　　　　　　　　　　　The TV show ended.
   (happened first)　　　　　　　　　　　(happened second)
   By the time

   _____

UNIT 8 Modals of Possibility

A ▶ Complete the sentences with the correct modals.

1. The train _____ (couldn't / might not) have arrived yet. It's not scheduled to be in for four more hours.
2. We _____ (couldn't / might not) have to cancel the picnic. It looks like the sun is coming out.
3. You _____ (may not / could not) believe this, but I lost 15 pounds in two weeks.
4. We _____ (could / couldn't) go to dinner after the movie. But that would be a little late.
5. My mother _____ (may have / couldn't have) gone to the library. It's open tonight until 9:00.
6. That job _____ (could / may) look difficult, but I don't think it will take that long.

B ▶ Complete the sentences with your own ideas.

1. I couldn't have forgotten _____.
2. My boss might _____.
3. I might not _____ tomorrow.
4. I may not be able to _____.
5. I could help _____ with _____ this weekend.
6. _____ may look easy, but it's actually difficult.
7. My friend couldn't have meant it when he said I was _____.
8. If it rains this weekend, I might _____.
9. If the weather is good this weekend, I might _____.
10. I couldn't study tonight because _____.

UNIT 9 Restrictive Adjective Clauses

A ▶ Complete the dialogue with *that* or *who*. Then underline the adjective clauses and circle the nouns that the adjective clauses describe.

A: What do you want to do tonight?

B: Let's go to the movie _____ your father told us about.
                              1

A: Oh, someone else told me it's really sad. I like movies _____ have happy endings.
                                                                  2

B: Who told you it was sad?

A: Megan. She's the woman _____ you met at the mall the other day. She works in my office.
                                3

B: Oh.

A: Anyway, we can see that movie if you want to.

B: No, never mind. Let's just go to dinner. Afterwards, we can watch the DVD _____ we got yesterday.
                                                                                    4

A: Good idea. And Chinese food sounds good.

B: Let's go to Nice Rice.

A: I haven't heard of it.

B: It just opened. The man _____ owns Super Noodle owns it.
                                 5

B ▶ Combine the two sentences into a single sentence. Use restrictive adjective clauses.

1. Henry is a young man. He lives in the green house up the street.
   _____

2. The Rockets are a basketball team. They won the high school championship.
   _____

3. Brenda is a manager. Her staff all quit.
   _____

Unit 9   Grammar Expansion   **131**

UNIT 10 The Passive Verb Form

A ▶ Complete the news clips below. Use the passive form of the verbs.

1. A famous painting _____ (report) missing from the museum on Wednesday. Police _____ (call) to the scene. Visitors _____ (ask) to leave the building. Four museums _____ (rob) since April.

2. Two men _____ (take) to the hospital with injuries after their car _____ (hit) by a truck early this afternoon on Pebble Road. Witnesses _____ (question) by police. The driver of the truck _____ (no / hurt).

B ▶ Change these active sentences to passive sentences.

1. Paparazzi often bother celebrities.
   Celebrities are often bothered by paparazzi.

2. A South African miner discovered a large diamond.
   _____

3. Some celebrities pay assistants a lot of money.
   _____

4. Spiders frighten some people.
   _____

5. Firefighters detected a gas leak.
   _____

6. Students made the ice sculpture.
   _____

UNIT 11 Future Real Conditional

A ▶ Match the two parts of each sentence.

1. _____ If I need a ride home, I'll
2. _____ If you don't hurry up, we'll
3. _____ If crime in the area increases, we'll
4. _____ If you drink too much caffeine, you
5. _____ If you read to your children, they'll
6. _____ If you don't take care of yourself, you
7. _____ If we have enough money next year, we
8. _____ If you come to visit, I'll
9. _____ If you work for a big company, you'll
10. _____ If I don't go to bed now, I

a. might travel to Europe.
b. move out of the neighborhood.
c. won't be able to sleep.
d. might get sick.
e. be late.
f. show you around the city.
g. call you.
h. probably get good benefits.
i. won't be able to get up tomorrow.
j. learn to love books.

B ▶ Complete the conversation. Use the correct form of the verb in parentheses.

A: What are you going to do after graduation?

B: If I can _____ (find) a job, I _____ (work) as a computer technician. I had an
                 1   2
interview at a big company last week. If they _____ (offer) me a job, I _____ (take) it.
                                                 3   4

A: Great. I hope that works out for you. Is the job here?

B: No. If they _____ (hire) me, I _____ (have to) move to Houston.
                  5   6

A: But if you _____ (move) to Houston, I _____ (no / see) you again!
                   7   8

B: If I _____ (get) the job, I _____ (call) or email every week, and I _____
        9   10   11
(visit) twice a year.

UNIT 12 Reported Speech

A ▶ Rewrite the sentences using reported speech.

1. "I can go 48 hours without sleep," claimed Tom.

   Tom claimed that he could go 48 hours without sleep.

2. Julia said, "My boyfriend is completely heartless."

   _____

3. "This drug is still being tested," emphasized the doctor.

   _____

4. "You could rent a car for the week," suggested Ted.

   _____

5. The teacher announced, "Everyone passed the test."

   _____

6. "I'll return the book tomorrow," Stan promised.

   _____

7. Cindy complained, "This restaurant is terrible."

   _____

B ▶ Read the paragraph. Then write three things the bookstore manager says he likes about his job. Use reported speech.

   I manage a small bookstore. The job doesn't pay well, but I like it. I enjoy recommending books to my customers. Many of the people who come into my store shop here regularly. I know about their jobs, families, and interests, so I can help them find what they want. I also love my staff. I have energetic, good-natured, intelligent people. We have fun working together. We're almost like a family. I also like having a variety of things to do. I do most of our bookwork, write the schedules, and plan our promotions and displays. I also open boxes, decorate the walls, answer phones, and help out at the cash register. I do everything my employees do, when we're busy. I even vacuum at night and put books away. I actually like to clean and organize the store!

1. The manager says that he enjoys recommending books to customers.
2. _____
3. _____
4. _____

GRAMMAR REFERENCE

UNIT 1

A ▶ Questions in the Simple Present of *Be*

Yes-No Questions			Short Answers	
			Yes,	No,
Am	I		you are.	you're not.
Are	you		I am.	I'm not.
Is	he		he is.	he's not.
Is	she	too	she is.	she's not.
Is	it	late?	it is.	it's not.
Are	we		you are.	you're not.
Are	you		we are.	we're not.
Are	they		they are.	they're not.

Wh- Questions	Answers
What is your dog's name?	It's Sam.
Where is my math book?	It's right there on the table.
How are you getting there?	We are taking a cab.
Why is he so angry?	He hates when his boss screams at him.
Who are you talking to?	I'm talking to my aunt.
When are they leaving to France?	They're leaving tomorrow.
What are you doing for vacation?	I'm going to Mexico.
Where is she going so late?	Her mom is sick. She's going to the hospital.

B ▶ Questions in the Simple Present of *Do*

Yes-No Questions			Short Answers	
			Yes,	No,
Do	I		you do.	you don't.
Do	you		I do.	I don't.
Do**es**	he		he does.	he does**n't**.
Do**es**	she	feel hot?	she does.	she does**n't**.
Do**es**	it		it does.	it does**n't**.
Do	we		you do.	you don't.
Do	you		we do.	we don't.
Do	they		they do.	they don't.

Grammar Reference **135**

Wh- Questions	Answers
What do you do Saturday nights?	I go out with my friends.
Where does she go to school?	She goes to Brent College.
How do we get there?	We can take the train.
Why do you worry so much?	I don't want to fail.
Who does she look like?	She looks like someone famous.
When do they want to practice?	They prefer to practice after school.
What does he think about the show?	He thinks it needs some work.
Where does it say we have to cut our hair?	It says it right here in the contract.

C ▶ Questions in the Simple Past with *Be*

Yes-No Questions			Short Answers	
			Yes,	No,
Was	I		you were.	you weren't.
Were	you		I was.	I'm wasn't.
Was	he		he was.	he wasn't.
Was	she	too	she was.	she wasn't.
Was	it	late?	it was.	it wasn't.
Were	we		you were.	you weren't.
Were	you		we were.	we weren't.
Were	they		they were.	they weren't.

Wh- Questions	Answers
What was she upset about?	She missed her flight.
Where were you last night?	I was babysitting my nephew.
How was the party?	It was great!
Why were they late?	They got lost.
Who was that guy?	That was my old boyfriend.
When was the show?	It was two nights ago.
What were you guys talking about?	We were talking about the game last night.
Where was I supposed to sit?	You were supposed to sit with your class.

D ▶ Questions in the Simple Past with *Do*

Yes-No Questions			Short Answers	
			Yes,	No,
Did	I	feel hot?	you did.	you didn't.
	you		I did.	I didn't.
	he		he did.	he didn't.
	she		she did.	she didn't.
	it		it did.	it didn't.
	we		you did.	you didn't.
	you		we did.	we didn't.
	they		they did.	they didn't.

Wh- Questions	Answers
What did you do last night?	I went out with my friends.
Where did she go to school?	She went to Brent College.
How did you get there?	We took the train.
Why did you worry so much?	I didn't want to fail.
Who did you borrow that dress from?	I borrowed it from my sister.
When did they finish the job?	They finished it late last night.
What did he think about the show?	He thought it needed some work.
Where did she find that lamp?	She found it at a garage sale.

UNIT 2

A ▶ The Simple Present of Other Verbs

Affirmative Statements		
I	work	
You	work	
He	work**s**	
She	work**s**	most of the time.
It	work**s**	
We	work	
You	work	
They	work	

Negative Statements		
I	don't work	
You	don't work	
He	do**es**n't work	
She	do**es**n't work	most of the time.
It	do**es**n't work	
We	don't work	
You	don't work	
They	don't work	

Grammar Reference **137**

Yes-No Questions

Do	I		
Do	you		
Does	he		
Does	she	work	most of the time?
Does	it		
Do	we		
Do	you		
Do	they		

Wh- Questions

What sport **does** she play?
Where do you travel during the summer?
What type of music do you enjoy?
Why does he like that restaurant so much?
Who know**s** how much tax we have to pay?
When do they perform?
What time does the show start?

B ▶ The Present Continuous

Affirmative Statements

I	am		
You	are		
He	is		
She	is	swimming	in the lake.
It	is		
We	are		
You	are		
They	are		

Negative Statements

I	am not		
You	aren't		
He	isn't		
She	isn't	swimming	in the lake.
It	isn't		
We	aren't		
You	aren't		
They	aren't		

Yes-No Questions

Am	I	
Are	you	
Is	he	
Is	she	swimming in the lake?
Is	it	
Are	we	
Are	you	
Are	they	

Wh- Questions

When	am I	
Where	are you	
Why	is he	
What time	is she	swimming in the lake?
How	is it	
How much	are we	
How long	are you	
How often	are they	

C ▶ The Simple Past of Other Verbs

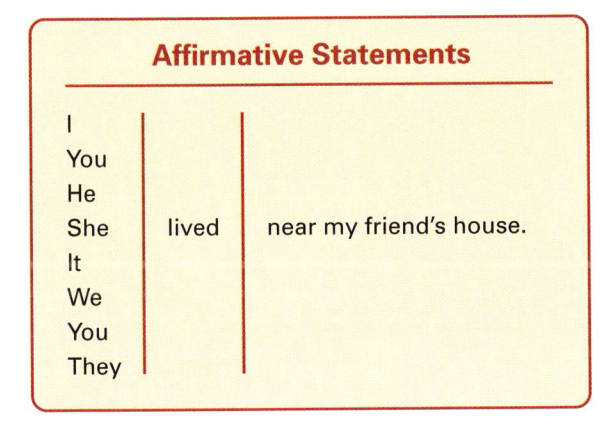

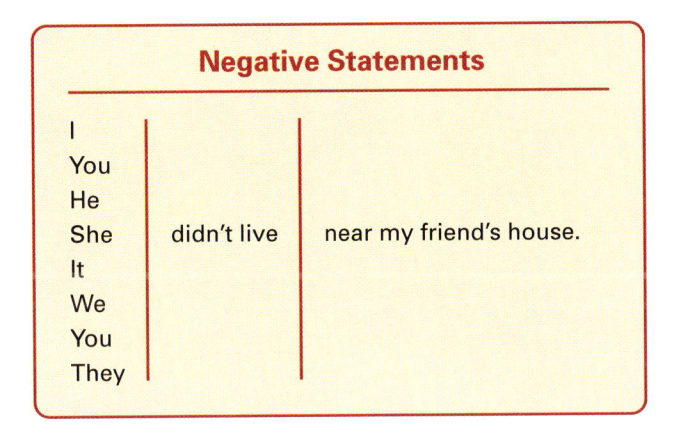

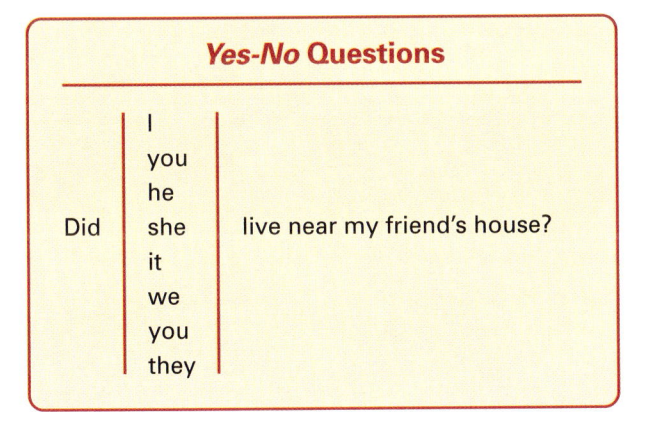

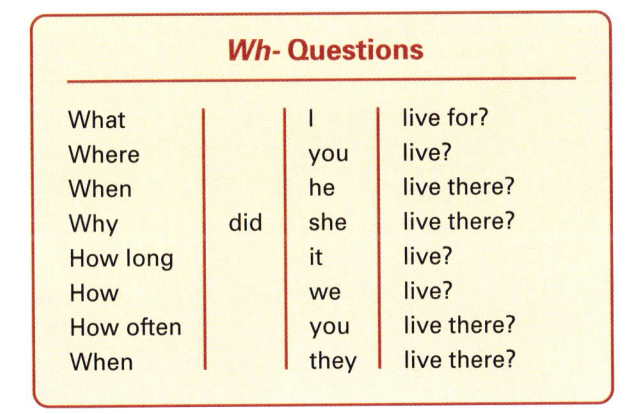

Affirmative Statements

| I / You / He / She / It / We / You / They | lived | near my friend's house. |

Negative Statements

| I / You / He / She / It / We / You / They | didn't live | near my friend's house. |

Yes-No Questions

| Did | I / you / he / she / it / we / you / they | live near my friend's house? |

Wh- Questions

What		I	live for?
Where		you	live?
When		he	live there?
Why	did	she	live there?
How long		it	live?
How		we	live?
How often		you	live there?
When		they	live there?

D ▶ The Past Continuous

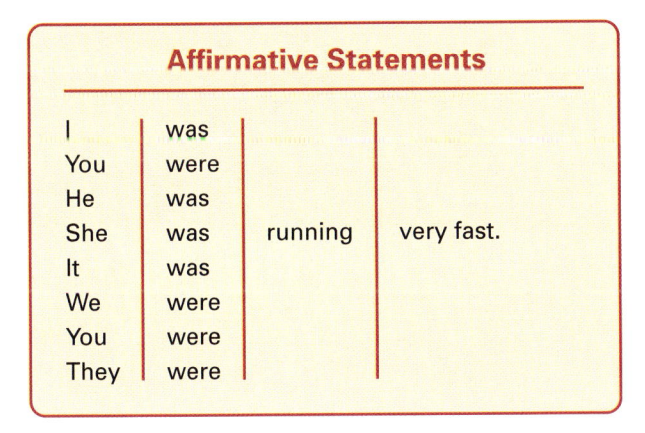

Affirmative Statements

I	was		
You	were		
He	was		
She	was	running	very fast.
It	was		
We	were		
You	were		
They	were		

Negative Statements

I	wasn't		
You	weren't		
He	wasn't		
She	wasn't	running	very fast.
It	wasn't		
We	weren't		
You	weren't		
They	weren't		

Grammar Reference **139**

Yes-No Questions		
Was	I	
Were	you	
Was	he	
Was	she	running very fast?
Was	it	
Were	we	
Were	you	
Were	they	

Wh- Questions		
When	was I	running very fast?
Where	were you	running?
Why	was he	running very fast?
What time	was she	running?
How	was it	running?
How much	were we	running?
How long	were you	running?
How often	were they	running?

E ▶ Irregular Verbs—Simple Past Forms and Past Participles

Base Form	Simple Past	Past Participle	Base Form	Simple Past	Past Participle
be	was/were	been	keep	kept	kept
become	became	become	know	knew	known
begin	began	begun	leave	left	left
bleed	bled	bled	lend	lent	lent
break	broke	broken	lose	lost	lost
bring	brought	brought	make	made	made
buy	bought	bought	meet	met	met
choose	chose	chosen	pay	paid	paid
come	came	come	put	put	put
cost	cost	cost	read	read	read
cut	cut	cut	ring	rang	rung
do	did	done	run	ran	run
drink	drank	drunk	see	saw	seen
drive	drove	driven	sell	sold	sold
eat	ate	eaten	send	sent	sent
fall	fell	fallen	set	set	set
feel	felt	felt	shake	shook	shaken
fight	fought	fought	shut	shut	shut
find	found	found	sleep	slept	slept
forget	forgot	forgot	speak	spoke	spoken
fry	fried	fried	speed	sped	sped
get	got	gotten	spend	spent	spent
give	gave	given	take	took	taken
go	went	gone	teach	taught	taught
grow	grew	grown	tell	told	told
have/has	had	had	think	thought	thought
hear	heard	heard	wear	wore	worn
hold	held	held	write	wrote	written
hurt	hurt	hurt			

Grammar Reference

UNIT 5

A ▶ Be Going to

I	am going to		I	am not going to	
You	are going to		You	aren't going to	
He	is going to		He	isn't going to	
She	is going to	stay for one hour.	She	isn't going to	stay very long.
It	is going to		It	isn't going to	
We	are going to		We	aren't going to	
You	are going to		You	aren't going to	
They	are going to		They	aren't going to	

B ▶ Will

I			I		
You			You		
He			He		
She	will	stay for one hour.	She	won't	stay very long.
It			It		
We			We		
You			You		
They			They		

UNIT 7

A ▶ The Past Perfect

Affirmative Statements

I		
You		
He		
She	had	over the puddle but
It	jumped	fell into it anyway.
We		
You		
They		

Negative Statements

I		
You		
He		
She	hadn't	the puddle and stepped
It	seen	right into it.
We		
You		
They		

Yes-No Questions

| Had | I / you / he / she / it / we / you / they | stayed | there all night? |

Wh- Questions

What		I	done?	
Where		you	seen	her?
When		he	talked	to him?
Why	had	she	disappeared?	
Who		it	bitten?	
How		we	reacted	to the news?
How long		you	worked	there?
How much		they	owed	you?

UNIT 10

A ▶ The Passive Verb Form

Simple Present

Affirmative Statements				Negative Statements			
I	am			I	am not		
You	are			You	aren't		
He	is			He	isn't		
She	is	taught	very well.	She	isn't	taught	very well.
It	is			It	isn't		
We	are			We	aren't		
You	are			You	aren't		
They	are			They	aren't		

142 Grammar Reference

Simple Past

Affirmative Statements				Negative Statements			
I	was			I	wasn't		
You	were			You	weren't		
He	was			He	wasn't		
She	was	taught	very well.	She	wasn't	taught	very well.
It	was			It	wasn't		
We	were			We	weren't		
You	were			You	weren't		
They	were			They	weren't		

Present Continuous

Affirmative Statements			Negative Statements		
I	am		I	am not	
You	are		You	aren't	
He	is		He	isn't	
She	is	being chased.	She	isn't	being chased.
It	is		It	isn't	
We	are		We	aren't	
You	are		You	aren't	
They	are		They	aren't	

Past Continuous

Affirmative Statements			Negative Statements		
I	was		I	wasn't	
You	were		You	weren't	
He	was		He	wasn't	
She	was	being chased.	She	wasn't	being chased.
It	was		It	wasn't	
We	were		We	weren't	
You	were		You	weren't	
They	were		They	weren't	

Grammar Reference

Present Perfect

Affirmative Statements				Negative Statements			
I	have			I	haven't		
You	have			You	haven't		
He	has			He	hasn't		
She	has	been	haunted.	She	hasn't	been	haunted.
It	has			It	hasn't		
We	have			We	haven't		
You	have			You	haven't		
They	have			They	haven't		

Past Perfect

Affirmative Statements			Negative Statements		
I			I		
You			You		
He			He		
She	had been	haunted.	She	hadn't been	haunted.
It			It		
We			We		
You			You		
They			They		

UNIT 11

A ▶ The Future Real Conditional (1st Conditional)

	I	run fast		I		
	you	run fast		you		
	he	runs fast		he		
If	she	runs fast		she	will get	to the park on time.
	it	runs fast		it		
	we	run fast		we		
	you	run fast		you		
	they	run fast		they		

144 Grammar Reference

I				I	run fast.
You				you	run fast.
He				he	runs fast.
She	will get	to the park on time	if	she	runs fast.
It				it	runs fast.
We				we	run fast.
You				you	run fast.
They				they	run fast.

UNIT 12

A ▶ Reported Speech

Direct Speech: "I think the teacher is absent."

I		I			
You		you			
He		he			
She	said (that)	she	thought	the teacher	was absent.
We		we			
You		you			
They		they			

Direct Speech: "I'm writing a letter."

I		I'm		
You		you're		
He		he's		
She	said (that)	she's	writing	a letter.
We		we're		
You		you're		
They		they're		

Grammar Reference **145**

Direct Speech: "I travel often."

I		I	travel	
You		you	travel	
He		he	travels	
She	said (that)	she	travels	often.
We		we	travel	
You		you	travel	
They		they	travel	

Direct Speech: "I shop when I feel sad."

I		I	shop		I	feel	
You		you	shop		you	feel	
He		he	shops		he	feels	
She	said (that)	she	shops	when	she	feels	sad.
We		we	shop		we	feel	
You		you	shop		you	feel	
They		they	shop		they	feel	

Direct Speech: "I collect stamps."

I	say (that)	I	collect	
You	say (that)	you	collect	
He	says (that)	he	collects	
She	says (that)	she	collects	stamps.
We	say (that)	we	collect	
You	say (that)	you	collect	
They	say (that)	they	collect	

Direct Speech: "It is time to go."

I	say (that)	
You	say (that)	
He	says (that)	
She	says (that)	it is time to go.
We	say (that)	
You	say (that)	
They	say (that)	

VOCABULARY SUMMARY

Unit 1
anonymous *(adj)*
celebrity *(n)*
exhausting *(adj)*
idol *(n)*
look up to *(v phrase)*
overrated *(adj)*
privacy *(n)*
underrated *(adj)*

Unit 2
condition *(n)*
cope *(v)*
face challenges *(v phrase)*
fragrance *(n)*
incident *(n)*
odor *(n)*
permanent *(adj)*
senses *(n)*
take precautions *(v phrase)*
temporary *(adj)*

Unit 3
aggressive *(adj)*
amazing *(adj)*
antisocial *(adj)*
compassionate *(adj)*
exhausting *(adj)*
frustrated *(adj)*
gentle *(adj)*
good-natured *(adj)*
patient *(adj)*

Unit 4
artist *(n)*
cartoonist *(n)*
chemist *(n)*
columnist *(n)*
cyclist *(n)*
economist *(n)*
environmentalist *(n)*
geologist *(n)*
linguist *(n)*
psychiatrist *(n)*
receptionist *(n)*
violinist *(n)*

Unit 5
come up with *(v phrase)*
exposure *(n)*
logo *(n)*
memorable *(adj)*
pay off *(v phrase)*
promote *(v phrase)*
slogan *(n)*

Unit 6
confident *(adj)*
depressed *(adj)*
gradually *(adv)*
patient *(n)*
treatment *(n)*
thrilling *(adj)*
unbearable *(adj)*
virtual *(adj)*

Unit 7
blame *(v)*
coincidentally *(adv)*
encounter *(v)*
impact *(n)*
thriving *(adj)*
transform *(v)*
triumphantly *(adv)*
vibrant *(adj)*

Unit 8
demanding *(adj)*
having a blast *(v phrase)*
opportunity *(n)*
permanently *(adv)*
sick of *(adj phrase)*
staff *(n)*
tiny *(adj)*
was dying to *(v phrase)*

VOCABULARY SUMMARY

Unit 9
imperfect *(adj)*
impossible *(adj)*
incapable *(adj)*
inconsistent *(adj)*
incorrect *(adj)*
unacceptable *(adj)*
unclear *(adj)*
unethical *(adj)*
unfair *(adj)*
unsuccessful *(adj)*

Unit 10
at risk *(prep phrase)*
compromise *(v)*
confidential *(adj)*
detect *(v)*
disgust *(v)*
get rid of *(v phrase)*
handle *(v)*
turned upside dow *(v phrase)*

Unit 11
assassinate *(v)*
grieve *(v)*
guidance *(n)*
inspire *(v)*
organic chemistry *(n phrase)*
premonition *(n)*
reveal *(v)*
scripture *(n)*
significant *(adj)*

Unit 12
angles *(n)*
aspects *(n)*
build *(v)*
cast *(n)*
crew *(n)*
fill in *(v)*
headset *(n)*
punching *(v)*

SKILLS INDEX

Critical Thinking

Agreeing and Disagreeing 91
Brainstorming 96
Comparing and Contrasting 2, 62, 68
Distinguishing Facts From Opinions 46, 82
Evaluating 60
Identifying Advantages and Disadvantages (pros and cons) 63, 96
Identifying Causes and Effects 91
Identifying Problems and Solutions 41, 52, 81, 121
Identifying Rhetorical Structure 8, 28
Integrating Information from Multiple Sources 11, 21, 31, 41, 71, 111
Listing 8, 12, 32, 52, 88, 96, 108
Making Inferences 6, 10, 22, 31, 40, 41, 62, 76, 81, 86, 90, 92, 100, 106, 121
Making Predictions 12, 16, 22, 26, 36, 66, 72, 82, 91, 92, 106, 113, 121
Paraphrasing 62
Ranking 51, 112
Sequencing 12, 23, 41, 53, 65, 66, 93
Summarizing 31, 50, 71, 72, 73, 78, 111, 120
Using Graphic Organizers
    Charts 28, 48, 52, 92, 96
    Graphs 48

Grammar

Dependent and Independent Clauses 34, 35
Expressions of Quantity 8
Future Real Conditional 104, 105
Gerunds and Infinitives, 24, 25
Modals of Possibility 74, 75
Quantifiers 54, 55
Questions in the Simple Present and Simple Past 3, 4
Passive Verb Form 94, 95
Past Perfect and the Simple Past 64, 65
Reported Speech 114, 115
Restrictive Adjective Clauses 84, 85
Simple Present for Future 44, 45
Simple Present, Present Continuous, Simple Past, Past Continuous, 14, 15
Time Expressions 64

Listening

Comparing and Contrasting 6
Distinguishing Facts from Opinions 46
Drawing a Conclusion 86
Listening for Advantages and Disadvantages 63, 96
Listening for Causes and Effects 103
Listening for Details 5, 6, 13, 16, 31, 32, 36, 43, 46, 56, 66, 83, 85, 86, 91, 95, 105, 111, 113, 115, 116, 121
Listening for Examples 56
Listening for Gist 16, 36, 51, 56, 111
Listening for Main Ideas 11, 16, 45, 56, 76
Listening for Opinions 21, 26, 36, 71
Listening for Reasons 6, 11, 21, 36, 51, 76, 81, 101
Listening for a Speaker's Tone or Attitude 76
Listening for the Best Summary 73
Making Inferences 6, 31, 41, 81, 86, 106, 121
Sequencing 41, 52, 65, 66, 93
Using Context Clues to Infer a Speaker's Feelings 76
Using Graphic Organizers
    Charts 83, 96, 105
Using Information that Was Understood to Guess Unknown Information 36
Using Prior Knowledge and Impressions to Make Predictions 26

Reading

Distinguishing Facts from Opinions 46, 82
Evaluating Summaries 50, 72, 78, 120
Guessing the Meaning of Words in Context 20, 30, 50, 52, 80, 90, 120
Identifying a Writer's Point of View 82, 118
Identifying Causes and Effects 102, 108
Identifying Likes and Dislikes 118
Identifying Problems and Solutions 52
Identifying Pronoun Reference 32, 60
Identifying Purpose 52, 90
Identifying Reasons 10, 30, 42, 61, 90, 92
Identifying Rhetorical Structure 28, 78
Identifying Sensory Words 38
Identifying Supporting Details and Examples 8
Identifying Tone 58
Identifying Topic Sentences 8, 18, 78, 108
Listing 8, 88
Making Inferences 10, 22, 40, 61, 62, 70, 92, 100
Making Predictions 22
Paraphrasing 62, 70, 110
Predicting 72, 86, 92
Ranking 112
Reading for Details 10, 20, 22, 52, 58, 80, 100, 102, 112
Reading for Answers to *Wh-* Questions 2
Relating to Content as You Read 112
Scanning for Specific Information 2, 42, 92
Sequencing 12, 23
Skimming for the Main Idea 12, 32, 72
Understanding a Character Description 98
Understanding Parenthetical Information 42

Skills Index **149**

Using Graphic Organizers
  Charts 28, 92, 102, 112
  Graphs 48

Speaking

Agreeing and Disagreeing 61, 77
Asking For and Giving Personal Information 15, 35, 46, 47, 55, 74, 77, 102, 105, 112, 113, 115, 116, 117
Asking for Additional Information 17
Asking for and Giving Advice 7, 27
Asking if Someone Has Time to Talk 57
Categorizing 101
Commiserating 27
Comparing and Contrasting 62, 68
Correcting a Misinterpretation 37
Describing Causes and Effects 91
Ending a Conversation 97
Getting to the Point 67
Giving Examples 25, 57
Interviewing 117
Applying Information in Different Contexts 11, 21, 31
Listing 12, 32, 52, 96
Making Excuses 87
Opinions
  Asking for and Giving Opinions 2, 7, 13, 17, 21, 23, 26, 31, 32, 41, 47, 51, 61, 67, 71, 81, 85, 97, 105, 111, 113, 116, 121
  Giving Reasons for Opinions 2, 13, 21, 23, 26, 31, 32, 41, 51, 61, 67, 71, 81, 113, 121
Paraphrasing 72
Predicting 12, 13, 16, 26, 36, 66, 82, 91, 106, 113, 120
Ranking 51
Restating Information 116
Showing that You Are Paying Attention 107
Speculating 117
Summarizing 41, 71, 72
Talking about Changes over Time 65
Talking about Problems and Solutions 41, 81, 121
Using Graphic Organizers
  Charts 107

Vocabulary

Adjectives for Personalities 25
Categorizing 25
Guessing the Meaning of Words in Context 20, 30, 50, 52, 80, 90, 110, 120
Negative Prefixes 85, 87
Using Suffixes 35
Words That Don't Appear in the Continuous 14, 15

Writing

Adding Information to Expand on an Idea 88
Agreeing and Disagreeing 51, 91
Describing a Process 88
Describing a Relationship 29
Describing Causes and Effects 108
Describing Changes 68
Describing Problems 108
Giving Reasons 88, 91
Mastering the Parts of a Paragraph 8
Narrating a Personal Experience 61
Opinions
  Supporting Opinions and Reasons with Details and Examples 8, 11, 29, 41, 51, 91, 101, 118
  Writing an Opinion 11, 41, 81, 101, 118
Shifts in Verb Tense 68
Summarizing 31, 41, 78, 111
Supporting Your Writing with Charts and Graphs 48
Using Graphic Organizers
  Charts 29, 48, 52
Using Punctuation to Convey Tone 58
Using Descriptive Language 38
Writing a Character Description 98
Writing Introductory Clauses 118
Writing Topic Sentences 18, 38

PHOTO CREDITS

Page 3: © Wang Leng/Asia Images/Jupiter Images; 4: © UPI/Landov; 7: © Masterfile (Royalty-Free Division); 9: (left) © WENN/Landov; 9: (right) © VCL/Spencer Rowell/Getty Images; 10: © Chip East/Reuters/CORBIS; 11: (left) © 2005 by Andreea Angelescu/CORBIS; 11: (middle) © AP Photo/Lauren Greenfield/VII; 11: (right) THE KOBAL COLLECTION; 12: (left) © lemonlight features/Alamy; 12: (right) © Steve Allen/Getty Images; 13: © Robert Warren/Getty Images; 16: © David White/Alamy; 19: (top left) © Elisabeth Cölfen/Masterfile; 19: (top center) © Royalty-Free/CORBIS; 19: (top right) © Zia Soleil/Getty Images; 19: (middle) © Jacques Cornell/MMH; 19: (inset) © Brand X Pictures/PunchStock; 19: (bottom) © Rolf Bruderer/Masterfile; 20: © Philippe Renault/Getty Images; 23: (top) © AP Photo/WLS-TV; 23: (bkgd) © Photo by Ron Nichols, USDA Natural Resources Conservation Service; 24: © Jose Luis Pelaez/Getty Images; 25: (top) © pierre bourrier/Alamy; 25: (middle) © Veronique Beranger/Getty Images; 25: (bottom) © Michael N. Paras/AGE Fotostock; 26: © Graham French/Masterfile; 27: © Marc Romanelli/Getty Images; 29: © 2007 Yellowdog Productions/Getty Images; 30: © THE KOBAL COLLECTION/UNIVERSAL/WORKING TITLE; 31: © 2006 Mark Parisi DIST by UFS INC.; 32: (left) © Reuters/Landov; 32: (right) © Eric Dreyer/Getty Images; 33: © AP Photo/Yves Logghe; 34: © Owen Franken/CORBIS; 35: © Bill Aron/PhotoEdit Inc.; 36: (left) © George Doyle/Stockbyte/Getty Images; 36: (right) © Michael Yarish/2005 CBS BROADCASTING INC. ALL RIGHTS RESERVED/Getty Images; 39: © REUTERS/Aladin Abdel Naby/Landov; 40: © Don Smith/Alamy; 42: (left) © Ian Arthur/Alamy; 42: (middle) © Jerzy Dabrowski/dpa/CORBIS; 42: (right) © vario images GmbH & Co. KG/Alamy; 45: © REUTERS/Mike Blake/Landov; 49: (top) © Estelle Klawitter/zefa/CORBIS; 49: (bottom) © REUTERS/Fred Prouser/Landov; 49: (background) © Nicholas Pitt/Alamy; 50: © Steve Vidler/SuperStock; 51: (top left) © AP Photo/Joe Imel; 51: (top middle) © Robert Harding World Imagery/Getty Images; 51: (top right) © Angelo Cavalli/zefa/CORBIS; 51: (bottom left) © Syracuse Newspapers/Al Campanie/The Image Works ; 51: (bottom middle) © Kevin Jordan/Getty Images; 51: (bottom right) © Dennis Macdonald/Index Stock/Jupiter Images; 53: © Courtesy of Dr. Hoffman; 56: © dpa/Landov; 57: (left) © Jim Craigmyle/CORBIS; 57: (middle left) © Royalty-Free/CORBIS; 57: (right) © Oote Boe Photography/Alamy; 57: (middle right) © Michael DeYoung/Alaska Stock LLC; 59: © Reuters/CORBIS; 61: © Big Cheese Photo/Jupiter Images; 62: (top) © Peter Vanderwarker Photographs; 62: (bottom) © Peter Vanderwarker Photographs; 63: (bottom) © José Antonio Jiménez/Superstock; 63: (background) © José Antonio Jiménez/Superstock; 64: © CORBIS; 66: © Astrid Stawiarz/Getty Images; 69: (left) © David R. Frazier Photolibrary, Inc./Alamy; 69: (right) © Yadid Levy/Superstock; 70: © Ariel Skelley/CORBIS; 71: (left) © AP Photo/Joe Raymond; 71: (middle) © JIM BOURG/Reuters/CORBIS; 71: (right) © Jeffrey L. Rotman/CORBIS; 73: (top) © Allison Barden; 73: (bottom) © Gerald Kooyman/CORBIS; 73: (background) © Norbert Wu/Getty Images; 74: © Courtesy of CReSIS Education; 75: © Matthew Richardson/Alamy; 77: © Clark James Mishler/Alaska Stock LLC; 79: (left) © Vienna Report Agency/Sygma/CORBIS; 79: (right) © Werner Nosko/epa/CORBIS; 82: © Jim Wehtje/Getty Images; 84: © Courtesy of Christina Santhouse; 85: (top right) © PHANIE/Photo Researchers, Inc.; 85: (bottom left) © Mauro Fermariello/Photo Researchers, Inc.; 85: (bottom middle) © Charles Gupton/CORBIS; 85: (bottom right) © Somos/Getty Images; 86: (top) © Lebrecht Music and Arts Photo Library/Alamy; 86: (bottom) © Image Source/Getty Images; 89: (left) © Lucianne Pashley/Superstock; 89: (right) © Brand X Pictures/PunchStock; 90: © AJPhoto/Photo Researchers, Inc.; 91: (left) © Brand X Pictures/PunchStock; 91: (right) © MIKE SIMONS/AFP/Getty Images; 96: © ImageState/Alamy; 102: © Jose Luis Pelaez Inc./Getty Images; 103: © Mary Evans Picture Library/The Image Works; 104: © Royalty-Free/CORBIS; 109: (top) © Brand X Pictures/Jupiter Images; 109: (middle) © Roy Morsch/CORBIS; 109: (bottom) © Chad Johnston/Masterfile; 111: © Mike Baldwin/Cornered/CartoonStock; 112: (left) © FOX SEARCHLIGHT/THE KOBAL COLLECTION; 112: (middle) © SuperStock, Inc./SuperStock; 112: (right) © Columbia Pictures Corporation/ZUMA/CORBIS; 113: (top) © Mark Leibowitz/Masterfile; 113: (top middle) © Comma Image/Jupiter Images; 113: (bottom middle) © Brad Wilson/Getty Images; 113: (bottom) © Royalty-Free/CORBIS; 114: © THE KOBAL COLLECTION/MGM/UNITED ARTISTS/SONY; 115: © Ryan McVay/Getty Images; 116: © Blend/Getty Images; 117: © David Young-Wolf/Photo Edit, Inc.; 119: (top) © AP Photo/HO/Courtesy of Rogue Pictures/Chen Jinquan; 119: (middle left) © Junko Kimura/Getty Images; 119: (bottom left) © THE KOBAL COLLECTION/

Photo Credits **151**

ROGUE PICTURES/CHEN JINQUAN; 120: (top)
© Adam Berry/Bloomberg News/Landov;
120: (bottom) © AP Photo/Elizabeth Dalziel.